DIESELS and ELECTRICS ON SHED

(Volume Five)

SOUTHERN REGION

DIESELS
and
ELECTRICS
ON SHED
(Volume Five)
SOUTHERN REGION

Rex Kennedy

Oxford Publishing Company

ACKNOWLEDGEMENTS

My thanks go to all who have contributed photographs and information for inclusion in this album, and especially to Colin Marsden and Brian Morrison who have been more than helpful and have, on many occasions, made special journeys to photograph locations and motive power for this particular volume. Sincere thanks also go to my wife, Pauline, who, particularly in the latter stages of the preparation of this book, spent many hours alone whilst I, and my son, Andrew, left home early in the morning, Sunday after Sunday, in an effort to fill the gaps and to complete the shed scene on the Southern Region.

Class 33/1 locomotive No. 33108 proudly stands outside Eastleigh Depot on 24th August 1978. All Class 33/1 locomotives are fitted with high level pipes for push-pull working with electric multiple unit sets, as can be seen in this view.

Colin J. Marsden

Half title page
Class 508 electric unit No. 50816 stands inside Strawberry Hill Depot on 5th March 1980. All new and refurbished stock is commissioned at this depot.

Colin J. Marsden

Typesetting by:
Aquarius Typesetting Services, New Milton, Hants.

Printed in Great Britain by:
Biddles Ltd., Guildford, Surrey.

Published by:
Oxford Publishing Co.
Link House
West Street
POOLE, Dorset

Frontispiece
A fine view looking down on the yard adjacent to Brighton Depot, showing both diesel and electric locomotives stabled on 8th November 1981. Locomotives include Class 73 electro-diesel No. 73123 and Class 33 diesels Nos. 33059 and 33019. Brighton's impressive signal box, and the viaduct which carries the line to Lewes, can be seen in the background.

Colin J. Marsden

Title page
One of the latest classes of electric multiple unit introduced to the Southern Region is the Class 455. The distinctive style of these units is portrayed in this profile as they bask in the sunshine at Dorking on 29th January 1984.

Rex Kennedy

INTRODUCTION

My fifth and final volume, depicting diesel and electric locomotives and units stabled and on shed, covers the Southern Region of British Rail.

Although this region is, geographically, the smallest of the five, it contains, together with its few interesting locomotive depots, many stabling points, especially those used by electric multiple units pending return to duty and, for this reason, this volume covers far more locations than any of the other books in the series.

The Southern Region's boundaries, and even the divisions, have, from time to time, changed considerably, with Weymouth, in particular, moving back and forth between the Western and Southern regions and, up to 1963, depots in the West Country, such as Plymouth (Friary), Exmouth Junction and Barnstaple Junction were under Southern Region jurisdiction. However, I have chosen to include only one of the West Country locations, Exmouth Junction, and this is shown below this introduction, otherwise this causes total confusion with the map of the region shown on the next page.

In this volume I have tried to capture the shed atmosphere of the Southern from the early days of diesels and electrics, when the prototypes were creating a great deal of interest, up to the present day, with the sophisticated Class 455 electric units and the attractively-named main line locomotives. One of the latest items of interest is, of course, the new 'Gatwick Express', with its regular service from Victoria, and every effort has been made to bring this book as up to date as possible, at the time of writing, and provide as much information as possible on the locomotives, units and locations.

In my research for this volume, I have been able to unearth a host of interesting facts for the benefit of the reader, and have tried to show, through the photographic content and captions, the various changes which have occurred over the Southern Region since its formation in 1948.

However, from an interest point of view, I could not resist the inclusion of a few pre-nationalisation and pre-grouping views such as those at Peckham Rye and Coulsdon North, and I am sure that these, too, will interest the reader.

Regarding the naming of locomotives on the Southern, I have included a section at Stewarts Lane showing various fine examples of locomotives and also some of the men responsible for the excellent preparation work carried out prior to the official naming cermonies.

In the late 1960s, when steam disappeared from the region, some depots had a sprinkling of diesel locomotives and as many of the old steam sheds as possible, such as Nine Elms, Feltham, Tunbridge Wells (West), St. Leonards and Basingstoke, have been portrayed with diesels on shed.

For those readers who have collected the entire *Diesels and Electrics on Shed* series, and for those with purely Southern Region interests, I hope this book will provide, both pictorially and in captions, useful information and will help them recall days gone by of the earlier diesel and electric scene, and the atmosphere, which cannot be described, which has always been there when visiting a British Rail depot anywhere in Britain.

Rex Kennedy
New Milton 1984

Although taken over by the Western from the Southern Region in 1963, after boundary changes, Exmouth Junction, in the early 1950s, regularly played host to the five prototype main line diesels, Nos. 10000, 10001, 10201, 10202 and 10203. These locomotives operated from here to the West Country towns such as Torrington, Barnstaple and Ilfracombe, which were then under Southern Region jurisdiction. No. 10202 is seen, on 20th August 1954, beside the water column, outside the shed building at Exmouth Junction beside 'West Country' Pacific No. 34024 *Tamar Valley*.

H. C. Casserley

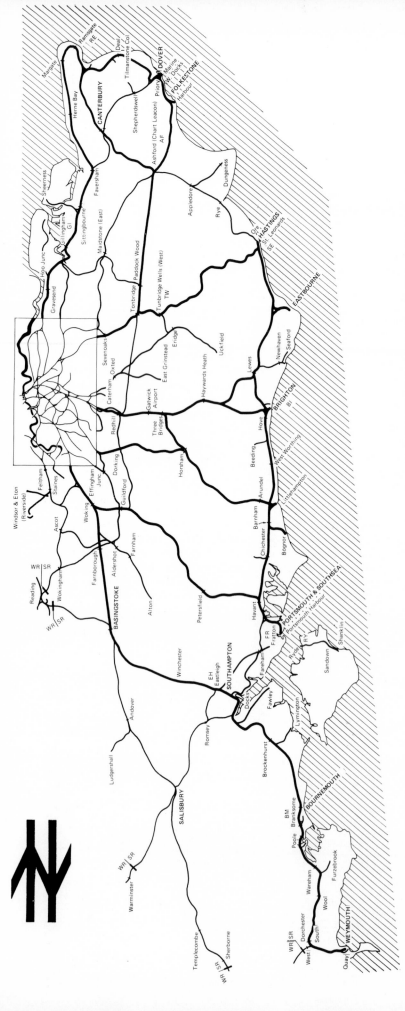

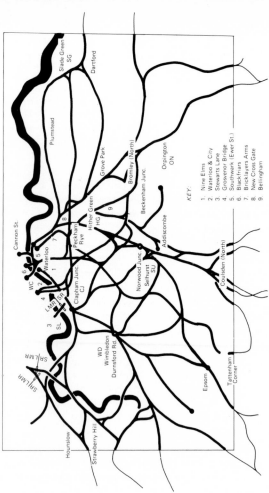

BRITISH RAIL
SOUTHERN REGION

showing regional boundaries, depots and fuelling points

BRITISH RAILWAYS MOTIVE POWER DEPOTS, FUELLING POINTS and STABLING POINTS of the SOUTHERN REGION, portrayed in this volume

SOUTH WESTERN DIVISION

Location	Code	Old Codes	Plates
Nine Elms Depot	–	NE/70A	1 – 2
Waterloo Stabling Point	WC	–	3 – 8
Waterloo and City Depot	CJ	–	9 – 12
Clapham Junction Stabling Point	–	–	13 – 15
Wimbledon E.M.U. Depot	WM/WD	WM	16 – 27
Durnsford Road E.M.U. Depot	–	–	28 – 30
Strawberry Hill E.M.U. Depot	–	FEL/70B	31 – 37
Feltham Depot	–	–	38 – 44
Hounslow E.M.U. Stabling Point	–	–	45
Staines E.M.U. Stabling Point	–	–	46
Windsor & Eton (Riverside) E.M.U. Stabling Point	–	–	47 – 48
Effingham Junction E.M.U. Depot	–	–	49 – 52
Woking Stabling Points	–	–	53 – 55
Guildford Stabling Point	–	GFD/70C	56 – 58
Guildford Depot	–	–	59
Farnham E.M.U. Depot	–	BAS/70D	60 – 61
Basingstoke Depot	–	–	62
Basingstoke Stabling Points	–	–	63 – 66
Winchester Stabling Point	–	ELH (Sub)/71A (Sub)/70D (Sub)	67
Eastleigh Traction Maintenance Depot	EH	ELH/71A/70D	68 – 96
Eastleigh Station Stabling Point	–	–	97
Fratton Traction Maintenance Depot	FR	FRA/71D/70F	98 – 104
Portsmouth & Southsea E.M.U. Stabling Point	–	–	105
Southampton Docks Depot	–	SOT (Sub)/71I/70I	106 – 108
Ryde (Isle of Wight) Depot	RY	NPT (Sub)/71F/70H	109 – 112
Sandown (Isle of Wight) Stabling Point	–	–	113
Bournemouth Depot	–	BM/71B/70F	114 – 116
Bournemouth Station Stabling Point	–	–	117 – 118
Bournemouth (Branksome) Traction Maintenance Depot	BM	71B (Sub)/70F (Sub)	119 – 121
Poole Stabling Point	–	–	122
Weymouth Depot	–	DOR (Sub)/82F/71C (Sub)/71G/70G	123 – 131
Weymouth Station Stabling Point	–	–	132
Salisbury Stabling Point	–	SAL/72B/70E	133 – 136

SOUTH EASTERN DIVISION

Location	Code	Old Codes	Plates
Stewarts Lane Traction Maintenance Depot	SL	BAT/73A/75D	137 – 167
Grosvenor Bridge E.M.U. Stabling Point	–	–	168 – 169
Blackfriars E.M.U. Stabling Point	–	–	170
Cannon Street E.M.U. Stabling Point	–	–	171
Southwark (Ewer Street) E.M.U. Stabling Point	–	–	172 – 173
Bricklayers Arms Depot	–	BA/73B	174 – 175
Peckham Rye E.M.U. Depot	–	–	176 – 179
New Cross Gate E.M.U. Stabling Point	–	NX/73B (Sub)	180 – 182
Slade Green Traction Maintenance Depot	SG	–	183 – 194
Plumstead E.M.U. Stabling Point	–	–	195
Dartford E.M.U. Stabling Point	–	–	196
Gillingham E.M.U. Depot	GI	GIL/73D/73F (Sub)	197 – 201
Hither Green Traction Maintenance Depot	HG	HIT/73C	202 – 221
Hither Green Continental Freight Depot	–	–	222
Grove Park E.M.U. Depot	–	–	223 – 225
Bellingham E.M.U. Stabling Point	–	–	226 – 227
Bromley (North) E.M.U. Stabling Point	–	–	228
Orpington E.M.U. Depot	ON	–	229 – 231
Sevenoaks E.M.U. Stabling Point	–	–	232
Tonbridge Depot	–	TON/74D/73J	233 – 234
Tonbridge Stabling Points	–	–	235 – 238
Tunbridge Wells (West) D.E.M.U. Stabling Point	TW	–	239 – 240
Tunbridge Wells (West) Depot	–	TWW/75F	241
Paddock Wood Stabling Point	–	–	242
Maidstone (East) E.M.U. Stabling Point	–	–	243
Faversham Stabling Points	–	FAV/73E	244 – 245
Margate E.M.U. Stabling Point	–	–	246 – 248
Ramsgate E.M.U. Depot	RE	RAM/74B/73G/73F (Sub)	249 – 252
Dover (Priory) Stabling Point	–	–	253
Dover (Marine) Depot	–	–	254
Dover (Western Docks) Stabling Point	–	DOV/74C/73H	255 – 258
Shepherdswell Stabling Point	–	–	259
Folkestone E.M.U. Stabling Point	–	FOL/74C (Sub)/73H (Sub)	260 – 261
Ashford Depot	–	AFD/74A/73F	262 – 266
Ashford Station Stabling Point	–	–	267 – 268
Ashford (Chart Leacon) Traction Maintenance Depot	AF	73F	269 – 273
St. Leonards Traction Maintenance Depot	SE	73D	274 – 278
St. Leonards Depot (original)	–	STL/74E	279
Hastings D.E.M.U. Stabling Point	–	–	280

CENTRAL DIVISION

Location	Code	Old Codes	Plates
Streatham Hill E.M.U. Stabling Point	–	–	281
Beckenham Junction E.M.U. Stabling Point	–	–	282
Norwood Junction Depot	–	NOR/75C	283 – 288
Norwood Junction Stabling Point	–	–	289 – 290
Selhurst Traction Maintenance Depot	SU	75C	291 – 298
Addiscombe E.M.U. Stabling Point	–	–	299
Epsom E.M.U. Stabling Point	–	–	300
Tattenham Corner E.M.U. Stabling Point	–	–	301
Coulsdon (North) E.M.U. Stabling Point	–	–	302 – 305
Caterham E.M.U. Stabling Point	–	–	306
Oxted E.M.U. Stabling Point	–	–	307
Redhill Stabling Point	–	RED/75B	308 – 311
Dorking E.M.U. Stabling Point	–	–	312 – 315
Gatwick Airport Stabling Point	–	–	316
Three Bridges Depot	–	3B/75E	317 – 321
Horsham Stabling Points	–	HOR/75D/75E (Sub)	322 – 325
Haywards Heath Stabling Point	–	–	326
Uckfield E.M.U. Stabling Point	–	–	327
Bognor Regis E.M.U. Stabling Point	–	HOR (Sub)	328
Barnham E.M.U. Stabling Point	–	–	329
Littlehampton E.M.U. Depot	–	–	330 – 331
West Worthing E.M.U. Depot	–	–	332 – 334
Brighton Depot	BI	BTN/75A	335 – 346
Seaford E.M.U. Stabling Point	–	–	347
Newhaven Stabling Points	–	NHN/75A (Sub)	348 – 349
Eastbourne E.M.U. Stabling Point	–	EBN/75G	350
Ore E.M.U. Depot	–	–	351

1 Although officially allocated to Nine Elms Depot for administration purposes, for a while Southern Region prototype diesel-electric 2-6-6-2 locomotives Nos. 10201, 10202 and 10203 were refuelled at Waterloo. These three locomotives, along with prototypes Nos. 10000 and 10001 worked double turns from Waterloo to Exeter and Waterloo to Bournemouth and included the 'Royal Wessex'. No. 10201 is pictured outside the depot at Nine Elms in the early 1950s.

Rex Kennedy Collection

2 No. D2179, a Class 03 shunter, later to be transferred to Eastleigh and Bournemouth, is seen 'off the rails' in the yard at Nine Elms Depot on 8th June 1963. The locomotive is in fine condition and clearly shows the BR lion emblem on the cabside. Nine Elms closed in July 1967 after an existence of around 119 years, and is now the site of the New Covent Garden fruit and vegetable market.

Colin Caddy

3 As mentioned in the caption to *Plate 1*, temporary fuelling facilities for diesel locomotives existed at Waterloo, by means of a tank wagon and fuel pipes as, in the early 1950s, only prototype main line diesels existed. In this view, on 29th October 1951, at Waterloo North Sidings, No. 10202 is seen being refuelled in this manner.

Les Elsey

4 Standing in what is termed the Hydraulic Sidings at Waterloo, on 7th August 1972, is Class 74 electro-diesel No. E6108, a locomotive which was converted from a Class 71 straight electric (No. E5005) in May 1968 for use on the Bournemouth electrification scheme. The locomotive was withdrawn in December 1977. These sidings get their name from the fact that the line leads to the hydraulic lift, seen in the background, which gives access to the Waterloo and City line.

John Scrace

5 At Waterloo North Sidings stands Class 73 electro-diesel No. 73106, on 23rd August 1977. This line is known as the 'coal road' and the old water column can still be seen beside the locomotive. When numbered E6012, this locomotive was one of the twenty two members of the class which were transferred from Stewarts Lane to Eastleigh in 1967, only to return to Stewarts Lane in 1968. The purpose of this transfer to Eastleigh was to assist with the Bournemouth electrification services.

Colin J. Marsden

6 On 14th March 1981, a variety of power lies stabled at Waterloo. Class 33 No. 33016 stands alongside the platform on the Hydraulic Sidings with Class 73 No. 73107, whilst in the six car electrified North Sidings is seen 4EPB set No. 5104 and 2EPB set No. 5785. The 2EPB unit is an ex-Tyneside set with the large guard's van.

Colin J. Marsden

7 Another ex-Tyneside set, no
Class 416/2 unit (2EPB) No. 579:
stands beside Waterloo and City c
No. S52, on 1st October 1982. Th
Waterloo and City car has just bee
brought to the surface by the use o
the hydraulic lift seen in the back
ground, to be pulled out 'by han
on to the sidings. The car is en rout
to Clapham for storage. No. 5792 wa
one of fifteen units, originally built fo
and used on Tyneside, which wer
transferred to the Southern Region i
1963. The black triangle on the un
denotes the brake van end of the train

Colin J. Marsde

8 On 26th May 1983, Class 33 No. 33008 *Eastleigh* stands in 'The Dock' at Waterloo, an area designated for stabling locomotives, and situated between platforms 11 and 12. The facade of this fine LSWR station can be seen in the background.

Rex Kennedy

9 The underground depot of the Waterloo and City line demands expert photography in the subdued light conditions. It is pictured on 28th September 1982 and shows views of a power car *(left)* and a trailer car *(right)*.

WATERLOO and CITY

Brian Morrison

10 Withdrawn Class 487 Waterloo and City cars await disposal in the depot beneath Waterloo Station on 28th September 1982. The Waterloo and City line operates to Bank Station in the City of London with up to five cars in each set, but with less cars in off peak periods.

Brian Morrison

11 A member of staff stands beside Waterloo and City car No. S59 in the depot on 8th October 1980. This car is a driving motor brake second, and these were introduced in 1940 having been built by English Electric. They operate on a third rail 600 volt d.c. system.

Colin J. Marsden

12 Waterloo and City driving motor brake second car No. S61 stands alone in the depot Cars are not permanently coupled and can run singularly.

Colin J. Marsden

15 With the new standard wrap-round livery, ▶ Class 50 No. 50036 *Victorious* waits at Clapham Junction stabling point on 12th August 1981, with empty coaching stock which will form the 16.38 Waterloo to Yeovil service.

Colin J. Marsden

CLAPHAM JUNCTION S.P.

13 The stock for all locomotive-hauled services from Waterloo is supplied by Clapham Junction. This view, of Class 73 No. 73114, shows the carriage shed and a Class 33 locomotive stabled in the background. Clapham Junction Station can be seen on the left of the picture.

John Eden

14 Another view of the stabling point and carriage shed at Clapham Junction. On 24th January 1980, a Class 421 (4CIG) unit, No. 7338, protrudes from the shed. The building on the right, with the circular white panels on the doors, is the CM&EE wagon repair shop.

Colin J. Marsden

17 A rare variety of units stand at the buffers at Wimbledon Park Depot on 7th September 1977. No. 001 is an old de-icing unit, whilst No. 6023 is a Class 414 (2HAP) unit. In the centre of the group stands No. 4002, one of the 4PEP 1972 prototypes to the high density units of today, which was developed into the Class 508. Coach No. 975207 is an ex-Class 501 unit which is used on development work, and last in line is No. 015, another de-icer.

John Scrace

18 A Class 418 (2SAP) unit, No. 5927, protrudes from the depot building at Wimbledon Park on 3rd December 1979. This unit was converted during 1976 from a 2HAP by changing the driver trailer composite cars to second class only use.

Colin J. Marsden

16 A general view of Wimbledon Park Depot with both SUB and VEP electric stock in abundance on 24th October 1982. The chimney of the Wimbledon Power House, which once overlooked this site, was taken down around 1959/60 (see Plate 27).

Colin J. Marsden

Departmental Units

19 Stores unit No. 023 offloads its equipment at Wimbledon East Depot on 9th May 1980. These vehicles travel all over the region to supply stores materials and equipment.

Colin J. Marsden

20 Departmental unit No. 051, which was converted from 2HAP unit No. 6156, is pictured inside Wimbledon Depot, on 29th May 1984, beside one of the new Class 455 units, No. 5814. No. 051 was used as a traction unit for 'Gatwick Express' stock and for ultrasonic axle testing, prior to its use with the high speed track testing car.

Brian Morrison

21 Although standing beside the tank of de-icing fluid at Wimbledon East Depot, on 25th August 1981, departmental test car No. 975027, formerly Class 501 car No. M61162, is not a de-icing unit. It is used for traction motor and bogie development.

Colin J. Marsden

22 A view of the carriage washing machine at Wimbledon Park Depot, with 4SUB unit No. 4628 passing through on 10th April 1981. These Class 405 units were withdrawn from service in September 1983 and were formed of four coaches with a driving motor brake second at each end. Some cars were introduced as early as 1946 and their workings were limited, being incompatible with any other class of electric multiple unit stock on the Southern Region.

Colin J. Marsden

23 Carrying the Wimbledon shed code on the front, Southern Region departmental unit No. 056, formerly experimental Class 455 (4PEP) unit No. 4001, is seen at Wimbledon on 3rd December 1979. This unit is now used for fitter training purposes.

Colin J. Marsden

24 On 18th August 1980, Waterloo and City car No. S56 undergoes repair in the lifting shop at Wimbledon East Depot. Generally speaking, these cars are usually overhauled at Selhurst Depot.

Colin J. Marsden

25 An interior view of Wimbledon East maintenance depot, showing Class 405 (4SUB) unit No. 4639 on 3rd December 1979. Wimbledon East Depot was improved to ease maintenance on Class 455 bogies, in 1983, and the depot is situated on the old site of Durnsford Road electric depot. Wimbledon Depot is responsible for electric multiple unit maintenance on the South Western Division.

Colin J. Marsden

26 Late in 1979, the Class 508 unit entered service on the Southern Region, and No. 508011 is pictured on 10th April 1981 inside Wimbledon East maintenance shed. The live 660—750V d.c. trolley wires can be seen hanging from the 'bus line' in the depot roof.

Colin J. Marsden

27 This view should be compared with that in *Plate 16* having been photographed twenty five years earlier. This shows Wimbledon Park Depot with the now-demolished Wimbledon Power House in the background, on 2nd March 1957.

R. C. Riley

DURNSFORD ROAD

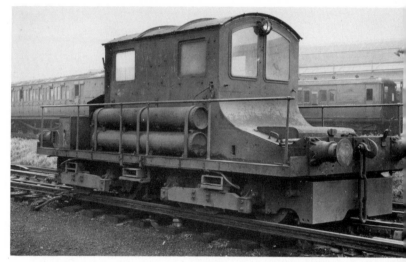

28 A very early photograph taken at Wimbledon (Durnsford Road), of an LSWR 3SUB electric multiple unit. Electrification of the lines in this area was announced by the LSWR in 1913, and the units were constructed at Eastleigh.

Colin J. Marsden Collection

29 Two of these unusual electric locomotives were used on the Southern, No. DS74 at Durnsford Road, pictured here in February 1957, and No. DS75, on the Waterloo and City underground line. They were built by the LSWR and operated by picking up current from the third rail (750 d.c.).

R. C. Riley

31 Strawberry Hill Depot sidings, on 5th March 1980, showing a newly-refurbished Class 411 (4CEP) unit, No. 411506, on the left, a new Class 508 unit, No. 508001, in the centre, and another refurbished Class 411 unit, No. 411608, on the right.

Colin J. Marsden

32 A withdrawn 2HAP unit, No. 6127, stands outside Strawberry Hill Depot on 5th March 1980. This unit was reinstated from scrap for CM&EE use at Strawberry Hill, but has now finally been withdrawn due to collision damage, as can be seen on the side panels.

Colin J. Marsden

◄
30 Durnsford Road Power-Station, Wimbledon, showing what is basically now Wimbledon East Depot, with units outside on 2nd March 1957, and the electric-powered shunter, No. DS74 on the power house ramp.

R. C. Riley

33 Southern Region departmental coach No. ADB975032 is seen at Strawberry Hill Depot, after conversion, in May 1976. This test coach is now named *Mars* and has a cab only at one end.

Colin J. Marsden
►

34 This interior view of Strawberry Hill Depot, on 29th May 1984, shows one of the new Class 455 units, No. 5833, standing over the inspection pits. No. 5833 is one of the first batch of Class 455 units, numbered 5801 to 5874. The first of the second batch, built with modified front end design based upon the Class 150 diesel unit, was delivered to Strawberry Hill on 20th June 1984, carrying the number 5701, instead of the expected 5901. The second batch is to include one ex-Class 508 unit TSO coach in their formation.

Brian Morrison

35 Two Class 416/2 (2EPB) units stand in the running and maintenance depot holding sidings at Strawberry Hill on 5th April 1980. The unit on the right carries a 4EPB sticker which is, in fact, wrong, and the units will soon be renumbered to 416788 and 416794, and are ex-Tyneside sets.

Colin J. Marsden

36 Class 411 unit No. 411510, and a new Class 508 unit, No. 508028, stand inside Strawberry Hill CM&EE Depot on 10th May 1980. The Class 411 unit has arrived from Swindon Works after refurbishing, hence the six figure number, and the Class 508 has arrived direct from York, where it was built. The vertical handrails on the 508 unit at the nose end are removed, and the 'via' blinds are taken out and replaced by destination blinds, before entering service.

Colin J. Marsden

37 On 10th May 1980, departmental test unit No. 4002 and 4CEP unit No. 7160 are seen at Strawberry Hill Depot. No. 4002 is one of three ex-4PEP prototypes, 2 x 4 cars and 1 x 2 car, and the 4CEP Kent Coast unit is en route to Swindon Works for refurbishment to return as Class 411 No. 1599.

Colin J. Marsden

FELTHAM

38 Feltham Depot was operational from about 1923, but was built in stages by the LSWR up to that date. This general view shows a solitary Class 33 diesel locomotive with sight of the six road shed which, at times in the 1960s, housed both diesel and electric locomotives.

Lens of Sutton

39 On 16th July 1965, Class 33 No. D657? stands proudly outside the old steam shed a Feltham. The depot closed to steam in 196? and, prior to that date, a small diesel depo to house shunters was erected. This ceased to be used, officially, from 9th August 1970.

Jim Astor

40 A Class 33 locomotive No. D6572 (now 33054) waits off duty at Feltham Depot on Sunday, 14th October 1962. This locomotive has since been fitted with snowploughs.

Gavin Morrison

Shunters at Feltham

41 On 20th August 1964, Class 03 shunter No. D2180 is seen at Feltham Shed. During the mid-1960s, the vast yards at Feltham were mainly worked by the larger Class 08 and 09 shunters.

Peter Groom

42 The Class 04 shunter could also be found at Feltham in the early 1960s and, on 9th June 1963, No. D2274 is seen beside one of the water towers in the shed yard. Feltham marshalling yard, a 79 acre complex built on Hounslow Marsh, was built towards the end of World War I, and was designed to place the entire freight operations of Nine Elms, Willesden and Woking at one location.

Peter Groom

43 The more familiar sight in 1967 at Feltham was the Class 08 shunter. No. D3462 is seen on 7th December 1967 in the very early blue livery, with wooden doors and the old style numbers. Upon closure of Feltham Depot, the entire shunter allocation was transferred to Selhurst.

John Scrace

44 Class 33 locomotive No. D6580 (later 33119) was the first of this class to be built as a push-pull locomotive, and was the only push-pull engine to carry the green livery. Today's observers will see that it now carries white window surrounds on its blue livery. It is seen here at Feltham, on 12th April 1963, in its original livery.

Jim Oatway

HOUNSLOW S.P.

45 Hounslow Stabling Point, a single line siding, normally used by only one train per day, is seen on 26th January 1980. A two car 2SAP unit, No. 5928 stands in the siding after working a parcels train from Waterloo.

Colin J. Marsden

STAINES S.P.

46 The stabling point at Staines, photographed on 1st February 1981. The units on view are Class 415/1 (4EPB) Nos. 5113 and 5121 and Class 416/2 (2EPB) two car set No. 5789. A Class 416/1 (2EPB) set No. 5671 completes the group. From 16th May 1983, the new Class 508 units were working to this location.

Rex Kennedy

WINDSOR & ETON
(Riverside) S.P.

47 The Southern Region's station at Windsor is Windsor & Eton (Riverside), where electric multiple units are stabled from time to time. On 5th March 1980, Class 414 (2HAP) unit No. 6033 stood off duty in the single line platform.

Colin J. Marsden

48 On 10th October 1981, a Class 415/1 (4EPB) unit, No. 5121 awaits its Monday morning duties at Windsor & Eton (Riverside). This fine station, designed by Tite as a royal station, is seen in the background together with Windsor Castle. The line runs from here to Staines.

Brian Morrison

EFFINGHAM JUNCTION

49 Effingham Junction is jointly shared by both South Western and Central Division units, and the shed building is earmarked for closure in the not too distant future. This general view shows four of the seven roads occupied by three Class 405 (4SUB) units and one of the later-designed Class 508 sets.

Colin J. Marsden

50 By 1981, Class 508 electric units were a familiar sight at Effingham Junction Depot, and Nos. 508022 and 508007 are pictured protruding from the shed building on 11th August 1981. This depot is used for off-peak and overnight stabling, in addition to the roof painting of units by the CM&EE Department.

Colin J. Marsden

51 Berthed for the night on 21st October 1980, when the 4SUB units were still to be seen in service, is Class 405 (4SUB) set No. 4618.

Colin J. Marsden

52 Wimbledon-allocated Class 508 unit, No. 508009, makes an impressive sight as it stands inside the depot at Effingham Junction on the night of 21st October 1980, after working a service from Waterloo.

Colin J. Marsden

WOKING S.P.

53 Woking (Hurdles Road) stabling point is situated adjacent to the station, and at week ends it generally offers a small selection of Class 33 and 73 locomotives. On 1st February 1981 Nos. 73130 and 73114 were to be found here together with Nos. 33021 and 33027 *Earl Mountbatten of Burma.*

Rex Kennedy

54 Photographed from a passing train is the inaccessible electric unit stabling point at Woking, which is situated beside the 'down' line north of the station. Class 423 (4VEP) No. 7822 and Class 414 (2HAP) No. 6077 are, on this occasion, amongst the two lines of units stabled.

Brian Morrison

55 Further down the yard to the south of Woking Station, on 1st February 1981, is stabled Class 33 No. 33005, the sun highlighting the bogie details of this 77 tonne locomotive. Near this point, the Guildford line branches away south from the main Waterloo to Southampton line.

Rex Kennedy

GUILDFORD

56 Locomotives are occasionally stabled at the south end of Guildford Station on the 'down' side. On 24th November 1980, Class 33/1 No. 33111 is seen at this location and is standing by for use in assisting long or heavy trains up the bank between Guildford and Redhill, at its steepest, an incline of 1 in 96. No. 33111 is fitted for push-pull working with electric multiple units.

Colin J. Marsden

57 On 8th January 1980, Class 33/0 No. 33012 waits at the more frequently used stabling point at Guildford. Behind this locomotive is seen a Class 415 (4EPB) unit, No. 5113, which has failed. No. 33012 was the first Class 33 to be outshopped from Eastleigh in the new livery, on 2nd December 1982, carrying the wrap-round yellow ends, black window surrounds and grey roof, although still carrying the small BR emblem and numbers.

Andrew French

58 Hauling damaged Class 117 Pressed Steel motor second car No. W51404 of set L424, on 27th September 1983, Class 33 locomotive No. 33043 is seen about to leave Guildford stabling point while en route from Selhurst to Swindon Works for repairs to be carried out. Only diesel multiple units on the Western and Scottish regions are marshalled in fixed formations, and Western Region sets carry a three figure number at each end of the set, preceded by a letter; L indicating the London Area.

Colin J. Marsden

The Shed

59 The old steam shed, situated between the station and the 845 yd. Chalk Tunnel at Guildford, during the depot's final days before closure in July 1967, saw diesel locomotives intermingled with the last of Southern steam. On 26th March 1966, Class 33 No. D6524 stands on the turntable which guarded entry to this half-roundhouse. The shed was opened by the LSWR in 1887 and now forms one of the station car-parks.

Rex Kennedy Collection

FARNHAM

60 The long five road electric multiple unit depot at Farnham stands on the 'up' side of the branch from Alton. This line once continued to Butts Junction, just beyond Alton, where three routes converged, from Basingstoke, Winchester and Fareham. This general view of the depot was photographed on 11th March 1984 and the depot houses Alton line and Guildford to Ascot units.

Colin J. Marsden

61 Class 423 (4VEP) units Nos. 7845, 7819 and 7705 stand at the blocks inside Farnham Depot on 11th March 1984. Class 415/1 (4EPB) units can also be seen at this location.

Colin J. Marsden

62 The old steam shed at Basingstoke closed with the end of steam on the Southern in 1967, after an existence of 52 years. This view, photographed on 5th September 1966, shows a Class 33 diesel on shed, and 'West Country' Pacific No. 34013 *Okehampton* passing with the 'down' Bournemouth Belle.

Ray Ruffell

The Stabling Points

63 Basingstoke Station stabling point is pictured on 7th August 1979, with two main line diesels of differing classes competing for attention. Class 33 No. 33019 is accompanied by a Class 46 'Peak', No. 46019, from Plymouth (Laira) Depot on the Western Region.

Andrew French

64 Class 73 electro-diesel, No. 73115, pictured at Basingstoke stabling point, was cut up after being involved in an accident on 6th January 1982 at East Croydon, whilst hauling an engineering train. It is seen in March 1978 together with Class 47 No. 47196, and has looped jump leads on one side only.

John Chalcraft

65 Another stabling point in the Basingstoke area is Barton Mill Sidings. On 24th May 1979, Class 73 electro-diesel No. 73110 was seen at this location stabled with stock from the 17.34 Waterloo to Basingstoke train. This train was locomotive-hauled for about nine months, due to shortages of electric multiple unit stock.

Andrew French

66 New Class 508 units stand at Basingstoke Yard stabling point, prior to entering service. At this time, February 1980, this location was being used for storage purposes.

Andrew French

WINCHESTER S.P.

67 Winchester, in the mid-1960s, used a small corrugated-iron shed for housing its Class 03 diesel shunter. No. D2085 is seen inside this small depot on 9th July 1967.

Roger Lamb

8 Eastleigh Depot was an interesting location for all types of railway enthusiasts in the early 1960s, with steam locomotives readily mingling with diesel traction. On 15th June 1963, the modern traction Southern Region classes were represented outside the depot; Class 33 No. D6595, Class 71 No. E5018, and Class 73 No. E6005. The Class 71 electric locomotive has either just left the works or is awaiting entry, as it carries no shoes or pantograph.

Les Elsey

9 Beside the concrete walkways at Eastleigh Depot, on 12th April 1962, No. E6003, a Class 73 electro-diesel, stands after being built in Eastleigh Works. Behind is a Class 33 diesel No. D6533.

Les Elsey

70 On 7th July 1981, a Class 3 locomotive, No. 33002 stands b side a 'Hampshire' Class 204 dies electric multiple unit, No. 140 inside the CM&EE depot at Eas leigh. No. 1404 is one of only fou units in this class which was forme from various Class 205 and 20 units, and the motors are clearl visible in this view.

Colin J. Marsde

71 On 27th May 1983, Class 33 No. 33018 was seen supported by four 15 ton floor jacks, the locomotive having been lifted to change its bogies.

Rex Kennedy

72 Class 33/0 locomotive No. 33027 *Earl Mountbatten of Burma*, complete with snowploughs, stands over the inspection pits, on 27th May 1983, whilst awaiting attention inside Eastleigh repair shops. The exhaust removing vents can be seen above the locomotive.

Rex Kennedy

Prototype

73 When this prototype diesel locomotive, No. 10201, was photographed at Eastleigh Depot on 12th February 1952 it must have created a great deal of attention amongst the many steam engines. It was one of three introduced on the Southern Region between 1950 and 1954, all eventually being broken up by Cashmores in 1968. Nos. 10201 and 10202 were, in fact, serviced at Eastleigh, but No. 10203 was generally serviced at Brighton.

Les Elsey

74 A view of the then recently completed extension to the diesel electric multiple unit depot at Eastleigh, which provided accommodation for control room and cable maintenance staff. Pictured inside the depot is a Class 205 'Hampshire' unit, No. 1122, with a Class 03 shunter, No. D2083, nearby, standing over the inspection pit.

Alan D. Baker

75 A Class 33/2 'Slim Line' locomotive, No. 33206, is seen inside Eastleigh Depot on 27th May 1983. These locomotives work on the Hastings line as the narrow Bopeep and Mountfield tunnels are difficult to accommodate the standard width locomotives, having only about ½ inch clearance to spare.

Rex Kennedy

Class 71

76 Class 71 straight electric locomotive No. E5004 (later 71004) stands on the shed at Eastleigh on 17th April 1967. These overhead pick-up locomotives only appeared on this depot after works overhaul, before being returned to the South Eastern Division where they operated. In 1961, experiments with small modified windows on the bodysides were tried out on these locomotives, in place of the former ventilating grilles, and No. E5004 was the first to receive this treatment.

John Scrace

Class 73

77 Also on 17th April 1967, No. E6004, a Class 73/0 (JA) electro-diesel, is pictured at Eastleigh Depot. The JA is instantly recognisable from the JB as it has an additional multiple control jumper beneath the driver's window, and an additional side window.

John Scrace

Class 74

78 The Class 74 electro-diesels were converted from ten Class 71 straight electrics, for use on the Bournemouth electrification scheme. No. E6102 (later 74002), pictured at Eastleigh on 25th July 1972, in its former state carried the number E5016, and was taken into stock as a Class 74 on 13th November 1967 and withdrawn on 8th July 1977.

John Scrace

Shunters at Eastleigh

79 This Class 04 shunter, No. 11222 (later to become D2252) was built by the Drewry Company and fitted with a Gardner engine. This class of shunter worked on all regions of British Rail except the Scottish, and No. 11222 is pictured at Eastleigh Depot. It spent its final working days at Hither Green Depot and was finally broken up at Southampton.

Norman Preedy

80 Another Class 04 shunter, No. D2274, is seen at Eastleigh Depot on 7th May 1966. By this time the yellow and black striped warning panels, on the front of the locomotive, were in evidence.

Colin Caddy

81 On 7th March 1964, No. D3011, a Class 08 shunter, stands at Eastleigh, with No. 34101 *Hartland*, a 'West Country' Pacific, nearby.

Colin Caddy

82 Heading ex-Bulleid stock, and comprising a breakdown train, Class 03 shunter No. D2041 is seen at Eastleigh on 28th February 1968. This locomotive was withdrawn in February 1970 whilst allocated to Selhurst Depot, and was sold to the Central Electricity Generating Board for use at Rye House, Hertfordshire.

John Scrace

83 No. 15201 was one of three shunters built at Ashford by the Southern Railway in 1937, and they were originally numbered SR1 to SR3. It was withdrawn from service in December 1964 whilst at Eastleigh, where it is seen on 29th July 1963 and was broken up at Swansea. The building of these shunters was the first attempt to replace steam shunters by diesel traction in the Southern's marshalling yards.

Peter Groom

84 The Bulleid wheels on No. 15221 are clearly seen in this view photographed at Eastleigh on 22nd April 1968. This was one of the second batch of Southern-built shunters, this time totalling 26, and they were built between 1949 and 1952. All were withdrawn by December 1971.

Ray Ruffell

85 No. 08650, a Class 08 shunter, undergoes maintenance in Eastleigh repair shops on 7th July 1981. To avoid pollution, it sits directly below the exhaust removing vent, and this particular locomotive is fitted with both air and vacuum brakes, and high level pipes for carriage shunting duties.

Colin J. Marsden

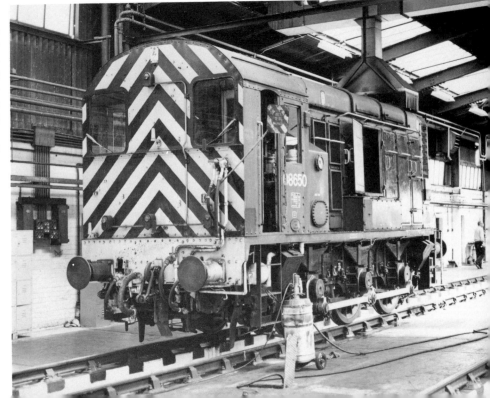

86 On the British Rail 'open day' at Eastleigh Depot on 30th April 1978, three Class 07 dock shunters were lined up alongside the depot. Nos. 07013, 07011 and 07005 clearly show the protruding door on the side, which gives access to the air compressors.

D. Kimber

Class 07
Dock Shunters
at Eastleigh

87 In its original green livery, Ruston & Hornsby 275hp shunter No. D2990 stands in the yard at Eastleigh Depot on 17th July 1962. It is noticeable that No. D2990 is not fitted with the high level pipes, as are all the others on this page.

Colin Caddy

88 On 10th October 1976, Class 07 No. 07011 (ex-D2995) is seen outside the depot at Eastleigh. Early in 1983, No. 07011, having been named *Cleveland*, was working with its former stablemate, No. 07005, at ICI, Wilton.

Brian Morrison

89 The London Transport electric locomotive *Sarah Siddons*, now preserved, was a guest at the 'open day' at Eastleigh on 28th May 1983. It is photographed the day before this event, having just arrived from London, hauling the green 4SUB unit No. 4732 *(see Plate 95)*. This locomotive, when in service with London Transport, was based at Neasden Depot and worked between Rickmansworth and London.   *Rex Kennedy*

90 A most unusual visitor to Eastleigh, on 17th October 1981, was Class 55 'Deltic' No. 55015 *Tulyar*. It had hauled the 'Wessex Deltic' excursion, a circular trip from Finsbury Park, organised by British Rail and incorporating the Southern Region, and had arrived at Eastleigh for refuelling and a photographic stop for the train's passengers.   *Colin J. Marsden*

Units at Eastleigh

91 New 2H diesel electric multiple units, later to become Class 205 (3H) sets, line up, on 8th October 1957, at the comparatively new depot built to house these units at Eastleigh. They are numbered 1101, 1102 and 1111 and the conversion to 3H entailed the addition of a trailer car.

Terry Gough

92 On 26th July 1980, Class 414 (2HAP) unit No. 6005 stands at Eastleigh Depot on the sidings which are used for the transfer of stock from Eastleigh Works to the traffic department. When built, No. 6005 included first class accommodation and when converted to a 2SAP unit (all second class) it was renumbered 5905. It reverted to No. 6005 later (first and second class) and, by incorporating 2HAP unit No. 6040, now forms part of Class 413/2 (4CAP) unit No. 3213.

Rex Kennedy

93 The first Class 508 unit to take up service was No. 508008, seen here inside Eastleigh Depot on 17th October 1981. It is accompanied by Class 08 shunter No. 08060. All the Class 508 units are in the course of being transferred to the London Midland Region's Merseyrail system to replace the 1938-built Class 503 units which are scheduled for withdrawal, and some Class 508 units are already working on Merseyside.

Brian Morrison

94 The electric multiple unit of the future, the Class 455, was introduced in 1982 and is fitted with air-operated sliding doors. No. 5801, which now bears the six figure number 455801, was brought to Eastleigh for the 'open day' on 28th May 1983, and was photographed the day before in the carriage sidings.

Rex Kennedy

95 Also brought along for the 'open day' at Eastleigh on 28th May 1983 was the green-liveried 4SUB unit, having arrived behind *Sarah Siddons*. No. 4732 was out-shopped in Southern Green livery with shaded letters in October 1982 and afterwards could be seen operating on the Central Division. In October 1983, No. 4732 was condemned and stored at Brighton pending preservation.

Rex Kennedy

96 Withdrawn Class 74 electro-diesels No. 74005 and 74003 await their fate at Eastleigh on 26th July 1980. These two locomotives, prior to being rebuilt at Crewe from Class 71s Nos. E5019 to E6015, and E5006 to E6103 respectively, started life in 1958, and No. 74005 was the last of the class to receive minor repairs at Eastleigh.

Rex Kennedy

EASTLEIGH STATION S.P.

97 Main line locomotives are stabled at Eastleigh Station whilst awaiting their next turn of duty. On this occasion two Class 47s Nos. 47064 and 47199 were accompanied by two Class 33 locomotives, Nos. 33014 and 33061 (behind). The Class 47 locomotives that arrive at Eastleigh work in on inter-regional trains.

Colin J. Marsden

98 A general view of the electric multiple unit depot at Fratton. Classes on view include 423, 413 and 421. This depot supplies units for Portsmouth to Waterloo trains and the Brighton 'Coastway' route.

Colin J. Marsden

99 On 9th May 1980, Class 427 (4VEG) unit No. 7904, displaying the Rapid City Link Gatwick—London stickers, stands beside Fratton Depot building. These units have now been replaced on the Gatwick line by the new-liveried locomotive-hauled 'Gatwick Express' stock, and have had their stickers removed pending conversion back to 4VEP units.

John Scrace

100 A Class 414 (2HAP) unit, No. 6105, lies stabled at Fratton Depot on 6th November 1983. During this time, a large number of withdrawn 2HAP units appeared at Fratton and were reported to be en route for Swindon Works.

Rex Kennedy

101 Passing through the washer at Fratton, on 14th June 1983 is Class 423 (4VEP) unit No. 7756, which, together with No. 7755, was fitted with experimental windows entailing the removal of the top opening windows in the large panels, and replacing them with a large plate glass window.

Brian Morrison

102 On 30th April 1961, No. 93, a departmental unit, later renumbered 012, which was converted from a 3SUB motor coach, circa 1959/60, is pictured standing at Fratton Depot. This de-icer, in extreme weather conditions, laid the de-icing fluid from the inner bogie of the unit.

Terry Gough

103 Standing in the yard, situated away from the depot at Fratton, on 6th November 1983, is Class 205 diesel electric multiple 'Hampshire' unit, No. 1131. These units are used on the non-electrified lines of the Southern Region, and their allocation is split between Eastleigh and St. Leonards.

Rex Kennedy

Fuelling Point

104 The fuelling point at Fratton is situated adjacent to the station, and a Class 33/0 locomotive, No. 33033, is pictured at this location. The facilities are mainly used for locomotives operating the Portsmouth to Bristol services, and are a far cry from the early days of fuelling diesels, as shown in *Plate 3*.

Colin J. Marsden

105 Concrete walkways forming the stabling point at Portsmouth & Southsea Station are clearly visible in this view photographed on 6th November 1983. A Class 413/2 (4CAP) unit, No. 3201, stands on the near road. This unit was converted from 2HAP sets Nos. 6006 and 6009 and is used on the 'Coastway' line.

Rex Kennedy

PORTSMOUTH & SOUTHSEA S.P.

SOUTHAMPTON DOCKS

106 Southampton Western Dock was originally known as New Dock and the Eastern Docks were termed Southampton Old Docks. Fou Class 07 shunters, No. 2988, 2992 2994 and 2997 are seen stabled a Western Docks during 1972, an the view shows the differing end on these unique Ruston & Hornsb locomotives which were speciall designed to replace the steam shu ters at the docks.

Barry Nicoll

107 In the mid-1960s, both steam and diesel shunters could be found on Southampton Docks and quite a common sight was to see them side by side on Eastern Docks Depot. On 21st August 1966, USA 0-6-0T No. 30067 poses for this photograph together with Class 07 No. D2987.

Robert Pritchard

108 The first diesel shunter to arrive a Southampton Docks, for clearance tests to con sider the possibility of replacing the USA tanks was No. 13014, on 21st October 1953, but th first five Class 07s, Nos. D2985–9, did no arrive on the scene until 1962. All shuntin duties on the docks are now carried out by th train engines and no shunters are to be found This view shows Class 07 No. 07006 leavin the Eastern Docks Depot, on 30th June 1974 hauling another of the class which has two fla batteries and is 'dead'.

Barry Nicoll

99 From 20th March 1967, the use of ex-London Transport underground stock on the Isle of Wight took place. These took the form of two classes, 4VEC (Class 485) comprising four cars, and 3TIS (Class 486), three cars. This general view of the depot at Ryde (St. John's), on 13th June 1982, shows 3TIS unit No. 032 beside the station platform, and 4VEC unit No. 485041 protruding from the shed. On the far right can be seen car No. S93, which is used as a spare.

Colin J. Marsden

10 The interior of Ryde (St. John's) Depot, photographed on 3th June 1982, shows car No. 20, of set No. 485041, undergoing servicing. This car is a motor brake second and the view shows the centre air-operated sliding door open. The Isle of Wight stock was converted from fourth to third rail operation in the Wimbledon workshops.

Brian Morrison

112 The sole surviving Class 05 shunter carries out limited duties the Isle of Wight. No. D2554, pictured here at Ryde (St. John's) Dep on 19th May 1968, at that time carried the nameplate *Nuclear Fre* seen on the grille. No. D2554 has only a vacuum train brake, (air c trolled from the locomotive).

David Wo

114 At the end of steam, at Bournemouth, diesel locomotives cou be found mingling with BR Standards and Bulleid Pacifics on shed. Tl shed, seen here, dates back to the mid-1930s when the old LSWR dep was remodelled by the Southern Railway. It closed in July 1967. Class 33 locomotive is seen on this once very active depot on 21 March 1967.

R. A. Panti

111 Two spare cars, when not in use, are usually stored near the stone arch beside Ryde (St. John's) Depot. These are Nos. S93 and S10, and the latter is seen at this location on 22nd June 1974.

John Scrace

SANDOWN (Isle of Wight) S.P.

113 During off duty periods, the Class 05 Gardner shunter, now numbered 97803 after being taken into departmental stock in 1981, is stabled at Sandown Station. On 13th June 1982, the only diesel locomotive on the Isle of Wight was seen at this location. At the time of writing, it was destined to be withdrawn and replaced by an 03 shunter.

Brian Morrison

115 Prior to the electrification the Waterloo to Bournemouth lin and its new electrified servic which commenced on 10th Ju 1967, it was felt necessary to all cate six Class 47 main line diese to Eastleigh to assist with tl Bournemouth expresses. The were Nos. D1921 to D1926, ar No. D1923 is seen in this view, shed, at Bournemouth, togeth with BR Standard No. 73092 ar 'Merchant Navy' Class Pacific N 35013 *Blue Funnel*, preparing depart.

Gavin Morriso

BOURNEMOUTH

116 No. 10201, the Southern diesel-electric prototype, was hauled out of Ashford Works, on 17th November 1950, for tests after its construction. On 28th of that month it commenced actual road running, and soon after, it worked expresses on the London Midland Region. When allocated to Nine Elms Depot, together with its stablemates Nos. 10202, 10203, 10000 and 10001, it worked the 'Bournemouth Belle' service on Sundays, and it is pictured on 13th February 1952 on Bournemouth Shed after working the 12.10p.m. stopping train from Southampton.

Colin Caddy

The Stabling Point

117 As the electrified line terminates at the depot just beyond Bournemouth, diesel-electric locomotives, which are used to haul the Weymouth boat trains from Waterloo, are stabled in Bournemouth Station whilst the train continues to Weymouth behind a Class 33 locomotive. The siding pictured here is often used for stabling the Class 73s, and No. 73103 is seen on 22nd July 1983. The engine will wait at this location for approximately five hours before returning with the 'up' boat train to Waterloo. The car-park in the background is on the site of the old steam shed yard.

Rex Kennedy

118 Preparing to take the next train from Waterloo to Poole and Weymouth, on 27th August 1980, is Class 33 locomotive No. 33114. Locomotives for this duty are, as can be seen, fitted with high level pipes and control jumpers to be used in conjunction with electric multiple unit stock. The twelve coach trains from Waterloo are separated at Bournemouth and four or eight coaches are locomotive-hauled to their destination at Weymouth.

Rex Kennedy

BOURNEMOUTH (Branksome)

119 The electric multiple unit depot at Bournemouth (Branksome) rarely sees a locomotive but, on 23rd March 1979, on the occasion of the visit of Her Majesty the Queen and His Royal Highness the Duke of Edinburgh to Poole, Class 47 No. 47539 is pictured reversing the empty 'Royal Train' stock into the depot.

A. J. Gwynne

120 Southern Region de-icing unit No. 001 is pictured stabled at Bournemouth (Branksome) Depot on 8th April 1977. This area was once the Somerset and Dorset line's approach to Bournemouth (West) Station prior to its demise in 1966.

David Habgood

121 On Sunday, 10th June 1984, Class 47 No. 47508 *Great Britain* arrived on shed at Bournemouth (Branksome) with the empty coaching stock of an excursion train. Above the nameplate it carried a 'GB' sticker, similar to that found on motor cars. The driver of the locomotive carefully glances back as he slowly eases his train under the cover of the shed. No. 3015, a Class 430 (4REP) unit, of the type used on the Bournemouth to Waterloo service, stands alongside. This photograph also gives a good view of the shed's structure.

Rex Kennedy

122 Locomotives are stabled on their trains to the west of Poole Station in a siding beside the 'up' line. Inter-regional trains from locations such as Manchester, Newcastle and Liverpool await their return at this point. In 1983, however, a new service operated between Waterloo and Brockenhurst and, to encourage visitors to Beaulieu, the 'Orient Express' stock was used, which was stabled at Poole pending its return journey. No. 33029 is seen on 11th June 1983 preparing to leave with the 15.00 e.c.s. Poole to Brockenhurst train. The first vehicle is the Gresley luggage van and the second, a BSK painted in the chocolate livery.

Andrew French

POOLE S.P.

WEYMOUTH

23 Weymouth Shed opened in 1885 and, during the last twenty years of its existence until it closed in July 1967, passed back and forth between the Southern and Western regions, staying eventually under Southern Region jurisdiction from 1958. After official closure of the depot, Class 33s No. D6544 and 6552 were seen on shed in August 1967.

David Habgood

124 The now preserved Class 35 'Hymek', No. D7018, is pictured at Weymouth Shed on 20th April 1962. These diesel-hydraulic 1,700 b.h.p. locomotives were introduced to the Western Region in 1961, having been built by Beyer Peacock, and sported the GWR style aluminium embossed numbers at each end on the cabside. These numbers were cast at Swindon Works and were then sent to Beyer Peacock for fitting.

Gavin Morrison

25 Class 33/1 locomotive No. 6528 (now 3111), fitted for push-pull working on the Bournemouth to Weymouth line, proudly stands outside the depot at Weymouth in December 1969. Alongside is seen a Class 120 Swindon-built diesel multiple unit, which would have worked down from the Western Region.

David Habgood

126 The last steam shunters used f
hauling boat trains from Weymou
Station to the quay, left for the We
ford Bridge branch, in Cornwall, c
23rd June 1962. However, after tria
involving No. D2292 in 1961, Class C
diesel shunters were already perform
ing these duties at Weymouth. N
D2180, complete with bell on th
front to warn pedestrians of its pre
ence, stands at Weymouth in Augu
1972.

David Habgoo

127 Although Weymouth officially
lost its allocation of locomotives in
1967, the depot building was still
used prior to its demolition in
1970. On 2nd August 1970, Class
03 shunter No. D2399 stands over
the pits which were once used for
the servicing of steam locomotives.

Norman Preedy

128 No. 15230, an early BR shunter, built at Ashford, is pictured on
shed on 3rd August 1967. For a
short while this locomotive was
used on the Weymouth Quay line,
after which time it returned to
Chart Leacon.

Colin Caddy

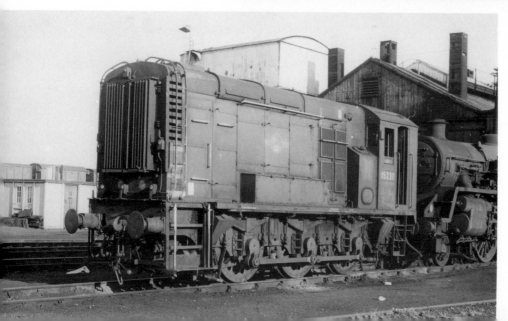

131 With the destination Maiden Newto
on the Western Region, on the blind, Cla
121 single car Pressed Steel diesel unit N
55032 stands in the depot yard at We
mouth in March 1965. This unit is no
allocated to Cardiff (Canton) and has sea
ing for 65 passengers.

David Habgoo

129 During its first few days in service, on 22nd July 1962, an immaculate Class 35 'Hymek', No. D7040, is seen on Weymouth Shed together with its classmate, No. D7019. This fine locomotive, resplendent in its green livery, has just worked a train in from Bristol.

Colin Caddy

130 One of the problems at Weymouth Shed was the servicing of multiple units, and Class 205 'Hampshire' diesel electric multiple unit No. 1127 is seen in the depot yard awaiting attention on 4th December 1966. The 'Hampshire' units were first used on services to Weymouth in the 1963 summer timetable, on Saturdays, from Eastleigh.

Colin Caddy

WEYMOUTH STATION S.P.

132 Since the dispersing of shunters at Weymouth, main line locomotives haul trains all the way to the Quay Station. During off duty periods, locomotives are stabled in the yard adjacent to the station and, on 7th August 1983, Class 33/1 No. 33105, sporting newly-acquired white window surrounds, sits in the sunshine at this location. Class 33/1 locomotives are fitted with a bell and yellow flashing light for the Weymouth Quay line, and this equipment is kept at Weymouth and fixed to the engine before proceeding down to the quay.

Rex Kennedy

SALISBURY S.P.

133 Locomotives are stabled adjacent to platform 5 at Salisbury Station and, on 11th December 1983, Class 33/0 No. 33001, and Class 33/1 No. 33109 fitted for push-pull working, are seen at this location.

Rex Kennedy

134 Three car 'Hampshire' Class 04 diesel electric multiple unit No. 1402 lies stabled at Salisbury Station on 11th December 1983. The present Salisbury Station dates from 1900–2, and lies to the west of the original station which was built in 1847. The old steam shed which, until the late-1960s, also housed diesels and, in particular 'Warships', was situated west of the station on the 'down' side of the main line.

Rex Kennedy

135 Class 205 (3H) 'Hampshire' units are used on the Salisbury to Portsmouth Harbour trains and No. 1105, with its black triangle denoting the brake van end of the train, is seen stabled in the siding just beyond Salisbury Station, on 11th December 1983. The line to Portsmouth Harbour, via Romsey, is not electrified.

Rex Kennedy

136 In January 1980, on the 'up' side of Salisbury Station, in the sidings behind the station, refurbished Class 411 (4CEP) unit No. 411510 was seen. This unit, formerly No. 7141, is en route from Swindon Works to Strawberry Hill prior to re-entering service, and is now allocated to Ramsgate Depot for working the Kent Coast line for which it was designed.

Andrew French

STEWARTS LANE

137 A general view of Stewarts Lane, photographed on 10th May 1959, and showing the electric depot on the left alongside t᎐ C&W maintenance depot. The roof of the old steam shed is on the right behind the offices, and beyond this, and out of sight, ᵃ the diesel servicing facilities. The electric multiple unit building is situated through the arches, also on the right, and a solitaᵗ Class 71 electric locomotive stands guard at the newly-built electric depot building, where current is picked up from overheᵃ wires, thus allowing electric locomotives to move freely within the depot, by using their pantographs.

R. C. Riᵣ

138 Three Class 73 electro-diesels, Nos. 73122, 73136 and 73101 *Brighton Evening Argus* are pictured outside Stewarts Laᵣ Depot on 11th July 1981. Also in attendance is Class 33 'Slim Line' locomotive No. 33207.

John Augusts₊

139 Carrying the BR lion on unicycle crest above the number, 0-6-0 Drewry shunter No. 11226, designated Class 04, awaits its next duty at Stewarts Lane Depot on 12th July 1958.

Jim Oatway

140 Stabled in the old fuelling siding, now only used for storage purposes, at Stewarts Lane Depot, on 26th November 1977, is Class 74 electro-diesel No. 74010. This locomotive was converted in 1968 from Class 71 straight electric No. E5021, being numbered E6110, and was withdrawn on 31st December 1977 after initially working in its new mode on the Bournemouth electrified line.

Colin J. Marsden

141 All Class 09 shunters are allocated to the Southern Region and all are dual-braked and fitted with an additional air compressor. They have a maximum speed of 27m.p.h. as against the 20m.p.h. of the Class 08 shunter. No. 09007 stands in the area which once formed the old steam depot at Stewarts Lane, on 7th February 1981.

Graham Wise

142 Preparation for the naming of diesel and electric locomotives is a long and rewarding task. The four men pictured here at Stewarts Lane, on 24th September 1980, are chiefly responsible for this duty. They proudly stand before their latest masterpiece, Class 73 No. 73142 *Broadlands,* and pose for a photograph. On this day, the nameplates were affixed to the locomotive prior to its official naming ceremony on the following day. No. 73142 is used for 'Royal Train' duties and official state visits.

Colin J. Marsden

143 The nameplate of Class 73 electro-diesel No. 73142 *Broadlands*, named after the home in Hampshire of the late Earl Mountbatten of Burma. The shields placed below the nameplate are the crests of the Test Valley (left) and the town of Romsey (right).

Brian Morrison

144 The official naming ceremony of Class 73 No. 73142 *Broadlands* was appropriately held at Romsey and, prior to this, the nameplates and coats of arms were covered when photographed on 24th September 1980. The locomotive is seen inside the depot at Stewarts Lane, after receiving final touches to the paintwork.

Colin J. Marsden

145 On 5th August 1981, a member of the staff of Stewarts Lane, Mr D. Sinclair, puts the finishing touches to Class 33/0 locomotive No. 33025 prior to it being officially named *Sultan* on the following day. A great deal of pride is taken in this work, as can be seen. The naming ceremony took place at Portsmouth Harbour Station and it was the fifth locomotive of the class to be named. Captain Austin Lockyer, Commanding Officer of the Royal Navy's School of Marine Engineering at Gosport, HMS Sultan, performed the ceremony.

Colin J. Marsden

146 The nameplate of Class 33 No. 33025 *Sultan,* showing also the decorative crest of the Gosport establishment. The crests, which appear on both sides of the locomotive, were manufactured in HMS Sultan's own foundry.

Brian Morrison

147 Class 33/0 No. 33025 *Sultan*, fresh from its repaint in preparation for its official naming ceremony, moves out of the depot at Stewarts Lane and into the sunlight. How long will the buffers remain white? Another of the class, No. 33050, stands in the background.

Colin J. Marsden

148 Last minute curtain adjustments over the nameplate of Class 33/0 locomotive No. 33056, *The Burma Star*, is carried out in Stewarts Lane Depot on 1st September 1980 prior to its naming ceremony. The paintwork is also being touched up in readiness for the big day.

Colin J. Marsden

149 The nameplate of No. 33056 *The Burma Star* is revealed on 1st September 1980, as it stands inside the depot at Stewarts Lane. Mr R. Jopp, together with the Southern Region Public Relations & Publicity Officer, make a last minute check that all is well. The Burma Star medal, awarded to those who fought in the Burma campaign from 1941–42, has been beautifully reproduced on the shield below the nameplate.

Colin J. Marsden

50 With snowploughs attached, on 1st September 1980, No. 33027 *Earl Mountbatten of Burma* is standing over the inspection pits inside Stewarts Lane Depot, prior to its official naming taking place. Lord Mountbatten, whom this locomotive commemorates, was uncle to His Royal Highness the Duke of Edinburgh and great grandson of Queen Victoria.

Colin J. Marsden

51 The new Victoria to Gatwick Airport express service commenced at 05.30 on 14th May 1984, with the new timetable scheduling trains every 15 minutes from 05.30 to 23.30. Class 73/1 No. 73123 *Gatwick Express* has been painted in the new 'express' livery, which compliments the refurbished rolling stock used on this service. It is pictured, on 9th May 1984, at Stewarts Lane, fresh from the paint shop, carrying both its new nameplate and headboard, prior to the official naming ceremony at Victoria Station. This fine looking locomotive not only took out the very first train of the new service, but is bearing the headcode GE ('Gatwick Express') and the novel adaptation of the BR crest, indicating its association with flight.

Colin J. Marsden

Royal Trains and State Visits

152 One of the more closely observed 'Royal Train' workings, carried out by Class 73 No. 73142 *Broadlands*, was the train which took the Prince and Princess of Wales to Broadlands at Romsey after their marriage in St. Paul's Cathedral, on 29th July 1981. The locomotive is pictured, in Stewarts Lane Depot, two days earlier sporting the headboard which carried the Prince of Wales' crest and motto, *Ich dien* (I Serve). The headcode carried was CD (Charles and Diana).

Colin J. Marsden

153 Another special working for No. 73142 *Broadlands* was the hauling of the train carrying Pope John Paul II from Gatwick Airport to Victoria, on his visit to Britain on 28th May 1982. The locomotive carried the standards seen attached to the front of the train and the headcode HF (Holy Father). Other state visits involving No. 73142 have included those by the late King Khaled of Saudi Arabia, the President of Nigeria and President Kaunda of Zambia. It was also used from Victoria to Tattenham Corner, on 2nd June 1983, for Derby Day.

John Scrace

Western Region Locomotives at Stewarts Lane

154 This Class 42 'Warship', No. 821 *Greyhound* has been cleaned at Stewarts Lane Depot in preparation for 'Royal Train' duties. These locomotives also worked over Southern Region metals from Waterloo to Exeter, via Salisbury, prior to the duty being taken over by Classes 33, 50 and 47. The locomotives that now work this service are maintained at Stewarts Lane.

John Scrace

155 Another Western Region-allocated locomotive, Class 50 No. 50045 *Achilles* is seen at Stewarts Lane, this time in the diesel fuelling bay. This locomotive is in the unrefurbished livery but refurbishment was carried out between March and August 1981 after original arrangements were cancelled due to No. 50010 *Monarch* being in urgent need of repair.

Colin J. Marsden

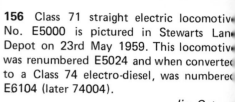

156 Class 71 straight electric locomotive No. E5000 is pictured in Stewarts Lane Depot on 23rd May 1959. This locomotive was renumbered E5024 and when converted to a Class 74 electro-diesel, was numbered E6104 (later 74004).

Jim Oatway

157 No. E5018, another Class 71 electric, stands off duty with a classmate in 1965. As ten locomotives of this class were converted to Class 74 electro-diesels, gaps naturally appeared in the numbers and it was found necessary to tidy up the list, causing No. E5018 to become E5003, with all numbers again running consecutively. The old shed code for Stewarts Lane was BAT (indicating Battersea) and Battersea Power-Station is seen in the background.

John Chalcraft

158 On 6th February 1978, Class 71 electric No. 71011 lies stored awaiting scrapping in the area of the old steam shed at Stewarts Lane. This depot closed to steam on 9th September 1963 and, as these overhead electric locomotives were introduced in 1958, this location held a great deal of interest for the enthusiast during the period 1958–1963, when both forms of traction could be seen.

Colin J. Marsden

159 In 1941, at Ashford Works, the Southern Railway built the famous CC1 locomotive, seen here at Stewarts Lane on 8th June 1963 and numbered 20001. It had both overhead and third rail pick-up facilities and was built for working heavy freight trains of up to 1,000 tons and also, together with Nos. CC2 and CC3, to work the Newhaven boat trains. This 100 ton locomotive was capable of hauling trains at up to 75m.p.h.

Colin Caddy

160 Class 73 (JA) electro-diesel No. E6005 (later 73005) is pictured at Stewarts Lane on 5th May 1963. The JA was built by British Rail at Eastleigh Works originally for use on the ex-South East & Chatham Railway lines.

Peter Groom

161 No. 73003, another Class 73 (JA) locomotive was, together with Nos. 73001 and 73002, originally built with oval buffers. These were later changed to the round Oleo pneumatic type, as seen here. The locomotive is pictured arriving at Stewarts Lane Depot, on 2nd July 1979, with a short train. The third rail, to accommodate electric locomotives, was installed in the yard in 1959, when the first electric locomotive arrived.

Colin J. Marsden

162 The electric multiple unit depot at Stewarts Lane, showing two Class 414 (2HAP) units, Nos. 6079 and 6070, and a Class 423 (4VEP) unit, No. 7868. The centre unit has the brake van at the end visible in this picture, as is indicated by the black triangle. The 2HAP unit was originally built to replace the ageing 2HAL units working on the London to Maidstone line, but they have now been converted into the 4CAP sets.

Colin J. Marsden

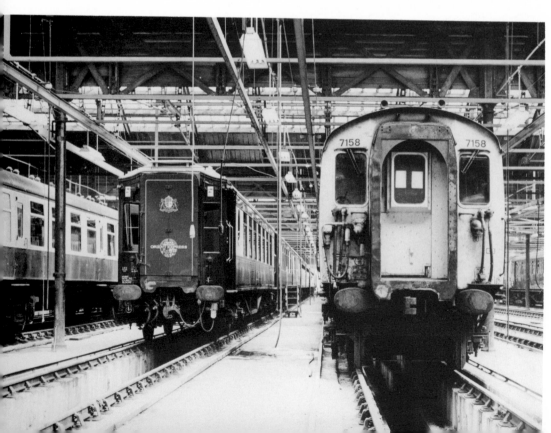

163 The 'Orient Express' (VSOE) stock is kept and maintained at Stewarts Lane Depot, and it is pictured here beside Class 411 (4CEP) unit No. 7158, standing over the inspection pits. The restoration of the VSOE was the brainchild of Group President James Sherwood of the Sea Containers organisation, to again provide luxury travel from London to Venice. In May 1982, the dream became reality and, in 1984, the fare for this memorable journey was £375.

Colin J. Marsden

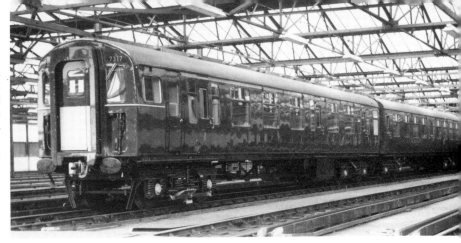

164 A green-liveried 4CIG unit, No. 7317, stands in the electric multiple unit depot at Stewarts Lane. These Class 421/1 units were introduced in 1964 and all were allocated to Brighton. Stewarts Lane Depot provides electric units for South Eastern Division services.

Colin J. Marsden Collection

165 The Southern Region General Manager's saloon, No. TDB975025, which was rebuilt in 1969 from 'Hastings' unit buffet car No. S60755, is pictured at Stewarts Lane Depot on 10th February 1982. The spotlights at the front end of this powered vehicle are used for tunnel inspections.

Colin J. Marsden

166 On 25th November 1979, the BR Board Research Department's ultrasonic test train stands beside the wall of the old steam depot at Stewarts Lane. This vehicle carries sophisticated track testing equipment.

Colin J. Marsden

167 To see a Waterloo and City car at Stewarts Lane is not a regular occurrence, as most repairs on these vehicles are now carried out at Selhurst. However, on 23rd March 1980, car No. S72 underwent bogie repairs inside the workshops.

Colin J. Marsden

GROSVENOR BRIDGE S.P.

168 Grosvenor Bridge stabling point is situated south of Victoria Station on the 'down' side of the line before the river. Togethe with the carriage sidings on the 'up' side, it provides accommodation for electric multiple units working out of Victoria. On 8th October 1983, two class 411/5 (4CEP) units, Nos. 1579 and 1569 are seen stabled.

Brian Morrison

169 Basking in the sunshine out side the covered accommodation at Grosvenor Bridge, on 26th July 1979, is motor luggage van No 68006. This is a dual-purpose vehicle and can work in mul tiple with any 1951, 1957, 1963 or 1966 type stock, front or rear as an additional van for parcels. It can also operate on non-electrified lines on its own or with a trailing load not exceeding 300 tons of vacuum-fitted stock.

Colin J. Marsden

LACKFRIARS S.P.

170 On 13th September 1982, Black-friars stabling point housed a Class 415/1 (4EPB) unit, No. 5184, seen here being passed by a Class 415/4 facelifted 4EPB unit, No. 5417, with the 11.22 West Croydon to Holborn Viaduct train.

Brian Morrison

171 At Cannon Street, electric units are stabled actually on the bridge which traverses the River Thames, and this view of a Class 415/1 (4EPB) unit, stabled on 31st July 1983, shows this very inaccessible location, photo-graphed from the river bank. Late in 1963, in a series of weekend oper-ations, this railway bridge was re-built to increase the span from 37ft. to 77ft. to make room for a dual-carriageway in Upper Thames Street. The operation lasted until April 1964.

Brian Morrison

CANNON STREET S.P.

SOUTHWARK (Ewer Street) S.P.

172 Since the demolition of Southwark (Ewer Street) Depot buildings, electric units are stabled at the location shown here on 13th September 1982. Class 416/2 (2EPB) unit No. 5758 stands attached to 4EPB and 2EPB units which have been painted in the new livery.

Brian Morrison

173 On 26th October 1979, the buildings at Southwark (Ewer Street) still stood and they displayed the nameboard 'Southwark Depot'. On this occasion, they provided a home for two Class 415/1 (EPB) units, including No. 5157. This stabling point is located on the South Eastern Division, south of the River Thames and west of London Bridge Station.

Colin J. Marsden

BRICKLAYERS ARMS

174 The famous clock of the old steam depot at Bricklayers Arms overlooks Ashford-built shunter No. 15234, seen at the depot on 11th September 1954. The lion on unicycle BR emblem and the Bulleid wheels on the shunter are clearly visible. This depot, once the principal shed of the South Eastern Railway, was opened in 1844 and closed to steam in 1962 after the first main line diesel duty had been introduced from the depot in the summer of 1960 using Class 33 locomotives. Until the early 1980s, modern traction could, on occasions, still be seen stabled at this location.

Brian Morrison

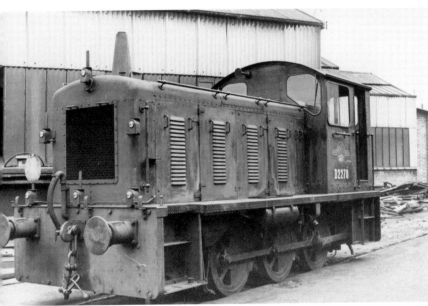

175 On 19th May 1961, Class 04 Drewry shunter No. D2278 is seen at Bricklayers Arms. This locomotive ended its working life, along with others of the class, in 1970, whilst allocated to Colchester Depot and was used at Ipswich Dock for shunting on the lightly-laid track after Ipswich had lost its own official allocation.

Jim Oatway

PECKHAM RYE

Pre-Grouping

176 Although photographed prior to Southern Region days, this fascinating scene at Peckham Rye Depot is worthy of inclusion. It shows LB&SCR Electrical Department petrol railcar No. 4, at the depot entrance, together with No. 1. Built by Dick, Kerr & Co., at a cost of £2,261 in May 1908, No. 1 became Southern Railway service stock No. 342S. In 1906, No. 4 was sent to Brighton to work the Kemp Town services, and was transferred to Peckham Rye in 1912 for use by the Electrical Department. Its Southern Railway number was 344S and both cars were withdrawn in 1931.

Colin J. Marsden Collection

177 Peckham Rye four road depot pictured on 28th February 1957. A 4SUB unit, No. 4511, protrudes from the post-war corrugated-iron depot. This 350 seat unit was reformed from LB&SCR stock and within it has ex LSWR coaches, one of only two in this class to include these vehicles, the other being No. 4501.

R. C. Riley

Bomb Damage

178 Completing the story of Peckham Rye by providing pre-grouping, post-nationalisation and, pre-nationalisation views, we see the result of an enemy air attack at the shed on 6th January 1945, and photographed two days after the incident. Southern Railway 4SUB units sit below the remains of the depot building, apparently unscathed at the ends of the trains visible in this view.

Colin J. Marsden Collection

179 It appears that the other end of the depot at Peckham Rye suffered the most severe damage from the air attack of 6th January 1945 as we can see from the ends of the units on view in this photograph; they appear to be damaged beyond repair. This devastating attack resulted in the depot being rebuilt in the form shown in *Plate 177*.

Colin J. Marsden Collection

180 A general view of the stabling point at New Cross Gate on 1st October 1983, showing the raised platforms, washer, and Class 202 'Hastings' sets Nos. 1013 and 1011 passing with the diverted 16.15 Charing Cross to Hastings train. Pictured in the lashing rain on the stabling point are Class 415/4 (4EPB) sets Nos. 5409, 5444 and 5411.

Brian Morrison

181 Southern Region units are also stabled near the station at New Cross Gate and, on 10th August 1979, Class 207 'East Sussex' diesel electric unit No. 1309 stands at this location. These units, built at Eastleigh, were introduced in 1962 for use on the Oxted line.

Colin J. Marsden

182 On 10th August 1979, a Class 421 (4CIG) unit, No. 7376, lies stabled with a 4SEP unit at New Cross Gate. No. 7376 was one of the third batch of 4CIG units to be introduced, being initially for use on the Waterloo, Reading and Guildford lines, to replace the ageing 4COR sets, but many are now used on the Brighton line.

Colin J. Marsden

SLADE GREEN

184 Slade Green car sheds, pictured on 8th November 1958. Two 4EPB units Nos. 5019 (lane 8) and 5198 (lane 13) bask in the sunshine with 4SUB unit No. 4696 (lane 9). This building was, in fact, the old steam shed which came into use in 1901, and the huge water-tower can be seen in the background.

R. C. Riley

183 An impressive view of Slade Green Depot, showing the mass of pointwork and lines of Southern Region electric units awaiting the call to duty. The line-up includes Class 415/1 and 415/2 (4EPB) units together with Class 416/1 (2EPB) sets. The scene was photographed on a Friday evening, and the majority of stock will be recalled to duty on Monday morning.

Brian Morrison

185 Class 508 unit No. 508011, pictured at Slade Green on 29th May 1981, was an unusual visitor to the South Eastern Division. This particular unit was the first of its class to receive general overhaul at Slade Green.

Brian Morrison

186 After over 80 years, the old steam depot at Slade Green is used as a running shed for Southern Region units and, on 6th February 1982, Class 416/2 (4EPB) set No. 5703 protrudes from the brick-built ex-LCDR depot. It was originally called 'Slades Green' but the 's' was soon dropped. Steam disappeared from here in 1926 when electric services commenced.

Colin J. Marsden

187 The London end of the multiple unit running depot at Slade Green was extended in 1959, resulting in a different style of structure to the original steam shed end. On 29th May 1981, units housed in this depot included Class 415/1 (4EPB) No. 5151, Class 423 (4VEP) No. 7770 and Class 416/2 (2EPB) sets No. 5718 and 5703, all having retired for the night.

Brian Morrison

188 With the water-tower in the background, departmental stores unit No. 024 stands beside the old steam depot at Slade Green on 4th May 1982.

Andrew French

189 During the evening rush hour, on 4th May 1978, the only unit in the running depot at Slade Green was this Class 415/1 (4EPB) set, No. 5148. This non-gangwayed stock was introduced between 1951 and 1954.

Brian Morrison

The Works

90 Slade Green Works undertake electric and general overhauls on Southern Region electric units and also on diesel electric multiple units. The idea to build a works for this purpose originated in 1924 and work was authorised in 1925, at a cost of £30,000. On 29th May 1981, a Class 207 'East Sussex' diesel electric unit, No. 1318, awaits attention outside the depot.
Brian Morrison

91 Inside the works at Slade Green on 6th February 1982, is Class 414 (2HAP) unit No. 6134. The unit is being stripped of all reusable parts, having been condemned, No. 6134 being one of the first to be withdrawn after legislation forbidding the use of the blue asbestos used on most of these units.
Colin J. Marsden

192 An exterior view of Slade Green Works, on 4th May 1978, showing Class 08 shunter No. 08600 prior to entering departmental service, and Class 414 (2HAP) unit No. 610_ taking advantage of the brilliant sunshine. On the far right is seen a Class 423 (4VEP) unit No. 7744, gangwayed throughout and awaiting attention. These express units are distributed between Bournemouth, Brighton, Fratton, Wimbledon and Ramsgate depots.

Brian Morrison

Ivor the Engine

193 Since entering departmental service, Slade Green's Class 08 shunter has been painted with broad red side panels and cab windows, with the panelling lined in white. This work was carried out at Stratford, on the Eastern Region, and also included the acquisition of its new number, 97800, and a name, *Ivor*. As can be seen, the area around the large-lettered name was later decorated with four painted daffodils. It is seen, soon after this 'repaint', on 29th May 1981, in Slade Green depot yard.

Brian Morrison

194 Slade Green Works, in addition to maintaining Southern Region multiple unit stock, carries out collision repairs to the region's locomotives. On 4th May 1978, Class 33/0 No. 33043 was pictured in the works after a collision at Nottingham on 11th October 1977. The unfortunate incident involved two locomotives, the second being No. 33036 which was condemned. The double-headed train, comprising 100 ton cement tanks, ran into wagons of a derailed coal train, and No. 33036 ran down the embankment into some unfortunate person's back garden. No. 33043 was recovered the following day.

Brian Morrison

195 On 15th April 1984, the stabling point at Plumstead was being used for the storage of vandalised units which were awaiting repair in Slade Green Works. This view shows the area well, the units stored being facelifted Class 415/4 (4EPB) No. 5402, and Class 415/1 (4EPB) No. 5110.

Brian Morrison

DARTFORD S.P.

196 A dismal day at Dartford, 20th January 1979, and stabled in the sidings awaiting a full Monday service are, along with other EPB sets, Class 416/2 (2EPB) No. 5768 and Class 415/1 (4EPB) No. 5185. After this rain came heavy snow, on 23rd January, creating the usual havoc on the region.

Brian Morrison

197 Gillingham Depot is situated on the 'up' side of the Ramsgate and Dover lines. This typically long depot building generally houses Class 415/1 (4EPB) and Class 416/2 (2EPB) Slade Green-allocated sets, and 4EPB No. 5319, fitted with express gear ratio, stands outside the depot on 9th January 1984.

Rex Kennedy

199 Beside the long depot building at Gillingham, on 29th January 1984, stands a Class 415/1 (4EPB) unit, No. 5360. As can be seen, three stabling lines are at this side of the depot and wooden platforms are provided for cleaning purposes.

Rex Kennedy

200 At the southern end of Gillingham Depot Yard are sidings with overhead lighting, where more units are stabled and, on 29th January 1984, three EPB units are seen facing north. They are Class 415/1 (4EPB) sets Nos. 5158 and 5232, and Class 416/2 (2EPB) unit No. 5723. Electrified services over the 78 route miles from Gillingham to Ramsgate commenced on 15th June 1959, using 4CEP, 4BEP and 2HAP units.

Rex Kennedy

198 Stabled at Gillingham beside the main line, partially beneath the washer, stands Class 416/2 (2EPB) unit No. 5715, with the brake van end towards the camera. A 4EPB unit, No. 5356, is also seen close to the entrance to the main line.

Rex Kennedy

201 Between the electric unit depot at Gillingham, seen on the far right, and the station, is a level crossing controlled by the signal box seen in this picture. The old steam shed was situated between this box and the station, and this depot closed to steam in 1960 following the introduction to the area of the Class 33 diesels. Motor brake de-icing vans Nos. 014 and 016 are pictured on 2nd April 1977 where the steam shed once stood. Mirrors for BR staff to view the third rail when de-icing is in progress are clearly visible.

Brian Jackson

202 This general view of Hither Green Depot, photographed on 2nd May 1959, shows the Class 24 Derby-built Sulzers lined u[p] beside the mass of ex-Southern Railway steam locomotives on shed. Of the first twenty Class 24s built, fifteen went to th[e] Southern Region in 1958 on loan from the London Midland Region until the Class 33s were available in March 1960.

R. C. Riley

203 This scene of 10th June 1961 shows the Class 33 locomotives now in attendance at Hither Green Depot, although the lowe[r] numbered Class 24s were still allocated to this depot until early 1962. Again we see steam engines completing the scene. The tw[o] diesels on view are Class 33 No. D6527 and Class 24 No. D5004.

R. C. Rile[y]

204 On 12th March 1960, two class 24s, Nos. D5001 and D5010, stand beside the fuelling point at Hither Green Depot. The initial use of this class of locomotive at Hither Green was on mixed traffic work in the Chatham—Faversham—Ramsgate—Dover area, prior to the Kent Coast electrification.

John Faulkner

205 The first depot at Hither Green was opened in September 1933, and was sited only 250ft. to the south-east of Hither Green Station. At the time this picture was taken, on 9th May 1959, a partition wall inside the shed divided the roads into two sets of three, one set for steam engines and the other for diesels. Again, Class 24s and diesel shunters are seen mingling with their steam stable-mates.

R. C. Riley

206 In 1962, Hither Green Depot became entirely diesel traction orientated and had full maintenance facilities. On 19th June 1966, No. D6562 is seen beside the old water column outside the depot. In steam days, roof vents were fitted to the depot *(see Plate 205 — steam side only)*, but these were removed subsequent to dieselisation.

David Wood

207 A more recent view of Hither Green Depot, on 11th March 1978, shows blue-liveried Class 33 locomotives in abundance including three 'Slim Jims', Nos. 33209, 33202 and 33205 and Class 33/0 No. 33035. Standing off duty is Class 08 shunter No. 08734 and the water-tower still overlooks the depot yard.

Brian Morrison

208 No. D6503, a Class 33/0 locomotive in green livery is seen at Hither Green in 1959. This particular locomotive was the one sent to Eastleigh in April 1962 for crew training as freight duties in that area were soon to be performed by this class of diesel.

Norman Preedy

209 The weeds now grow through the track at Hither Green Depot, but the basic structure of the old steam depot still stands. Guarding the entrance to the depot, on 9th October 1982, are Class 33 diesels Nos. 33047, 33202 and 33205 together with Class 73 electro-diesel No. 73123. This depot is scheduled for closure within the next two years when all its allocation will be transferred to Stewarts Lane.

Brian Morrison

210 Hither Green Depot was built to house locomotives mainly to be used on freight duties in Kent, and a large marshalling yard was laid at the same time. Class 33s perform most of the freight duties and these include the Class 33/2 'Slim Line' variety, all of which are allocated to Hither Green. However, on this occasion, two Class 33/1 locomotives, Nos. D6573 and D6579, stand outside the shed with departmental shunter No. DS1173.

John Chalcraft

211 Over the inspection pits, inside Hither Green Depot, on 9th October 1982, are Class 33/0 No. 33053 and Class 33/2 No. 33209. The headcode 'G6' indicates a Victoria—Nunhead—Chislehurst—Deal—Margate train, and '6E' indicates a train from Hither Green to Bricklayers Arms or Norwood, probably their last turns of duty.

Colin J. Marsden

212 On 5th May 1960, Class 04 Drewry shunter No. 11226 (later D2256) was pictured on Hither Green Depot, where steam was still in attendance. This depot received its first six green-liveried Drewry diesel-mechanical shunters, Nos. 11220–11225, by April 1957, and No. 11226 arrived later that year.

Peter Groom

213 No. DS1173 was the service loco at Hither Green during the 1950s and 1960s and was under the control of the Engineer's Department. Pictured here on the depot, on 27th April 1958, this 204b.h.p. five speed Drewry locomotive, was built in 1947 at Vulcan Foundry and, prior to its arrival at Hither Green, worked at Gorton, Manchester and in East Anglia. It was later renumbered D2341 and withdrawn in December 1968.

Peter Groom

214 Photographed off duty at Hither Green Depot, on 28th June 1959, is Class 03 shunter No D2083. This locomotive is vacuum-braked only and was one of the earlier members of the class to be withdrawn from service, in July 1969, whilst allocated to Eastleigh, but far outlived its steam companions seen nearby.

Peter Groom

15 One of the three Southern Railway-designed shunters built in 1937 was No. 15202, seen at Hither Green Depot on 27th April 1958. It was withdrawn on 24th July 1965 after 28 years service on the Southern, and spent its last days at Ashford, its birthplace. The original number of this locomotive was Southern No. 2.

Peter Groom

216 Seen at Hither Green Depot on 19th June 1966 is No. 15222, one of the second batch of Southern-built shunters which emerged between 1949 and 1952. This locomotive is fitted with the Bulleid wheels and, about this time, Hither Green had approximately nine of this class, originally comprising 26, allocated to its depot.

Roger Lamb

217 Class 08 and 09 shunters, the now familiar sight on the Southern Region, stand together at Hither Green Depot on 19th April 1981. Nos. 08653 and 09007 are now dual-braked. All Class 09 shunters now operate on the Southern Region, but for many years Nos. 09024 and 09025 operated from Allerton, Liverpool, on the London Midland Region.

D. Radusin

218 On 20th September 1980, the covered fuelling point at Hither Green featured in this view, and shows Class 73 electro-diesel No. 73131 with a Class 33 diesel locomotive. The Class 73s were found to be ideal for duties in Hither Green's marshalling yards as they were able to also operate under diesel power at 600b.h.p., whereas the Class 71 overhead electrics were less adaptable in situations such as this.

M. J. Howart

219 Three Class 71 straight electrics await their fate, on 11th March 1978, at Hither Green Depot. They are Nos. 71014, 71004 and 71009. The differences in ventilation grilles, which appeared on each side of the Class 71s, are clearly noticeable in this view.

Brian Morrison

Departmental Units

220 Hither Green is strictly a locomotive depot and the only units that appear on shed are from departmental stock. Former 2HAL unit, now numbered 022, caters for depot stores requirements and open pallets are fitted inside, in place of the seating. It has arrived at Hither Green, on 22nd June 1977, on one of its turns of duty.

John Scrace

221 Stores unit No. 024 was formed from redundant SUB units and, together with ex-2HAL departmental stores units Nos. 022 and 023 *(see Plate 220)*, operates a weekly schedule, supplying all depots on the Southern Region, and Eastleigh Works, with their requirements. Of particular interest in this view, photographed at Hither Green on 13th June 1978, are the shoe protection boards fitted to the concrete walkway, with the unit perfectly parked.

Colin J. Marsden

HITHER GREEN CONTINENTAL FREIGHT DEPOT

222 Hither Green Continental Freight Depot for perishable traffic, designed to deal with long wheelbase Dover to Dunkirk ferry wagons, was opened on 10th October 1960 and, when built, was capable of accommodating fifty wagons. It replaced the cramped and inconvenient Southwark Depot. Six sorting roads outside the depot were equipped with overhead wires to cater for the Class 71 electric locomotives, and these can be seen in this view, photographed at the depot on 29th September 1968. No. E5002 lies stabled in one of these sidings.

Robert Pritchard

223 Grove Park Depot is situated south of Hither Green on the Tunbridge Wells line, just over eight miles from Charing Cross Station. This depot came into full operation in 1962 and this view, taken on 1st April 1984, shows units deep inside the shed with Class 416/2 (2EPB) set No. 5762, and Class 415 (4EPB) sets Nos. 5134 and 5301 alongside.

Brian Morrison

◄

224 On 1st April 1984, units which stood in the carriage cleaning bay at Grove Park Depot included Class 414/3 (2HAP) set No. 6092, and Class 415 (4EPB) sets Nos. 5261 (408 seats) and 5323 (392 seats).

Brian Morrison

BELLINGHAM S.P.

226 There are two electric unit stabling points at Bellingham, just south of Catford and, at the northerly location, near the station, on 1st February 1984, Class 415/2 (4EPB) unit No. 5352 is seen. This non-gangwayed stock was introduced between 1960 and 1964.

Brian Morrison

227 At the more southerly stabling point at Bellingham, on 1st February 1984, more 4EPB units are pictured. Class 415/1 unit No. 5169 (introduced between 1951 and 1954) is seen beside the main line, whilst Class 415/2 units Nos. 5763 and 5721 make up the trio. The train in the distance is on a Holborn Viaduct to Sevenoaks service.

Brian Morrison

225 The interior of Grove Park's six road depot, photographed on 1st April 1984. Again EPB sets monopolise the undercover accommodation. Two Class 416/2 (2EPB) units, Nos. 5730 and 5728, flank Class 415/2 (4EPB) set No. 5306.

Brian Morrison

BROMLEY (North) S.P.

228 Bromley North Station is situated at the end of the line which joins the main line at Grove Park Junction. The branch opened on 1st January 1878 and is now controlled by the London Bridge panel. Platform 1, also used by service trains, is used for the stabling of units not in use. On 1st February 1984, three EPB sets, Class 415/1 No. 5187, Class 416/2 No. 5731 and Class 415/1 No. 5174, occupy this line.

Brian Morrison

229 Like the majority of location on the Sevenoaks line, Orpingto also generally plays host to EP electric units. The four road depo is situated beside the main line and on 5th February 1984, Class 415/ (4EPB) unit No. 5004 was seen o shed. Another unit of the sam class lies stabled further down th line in the 'up' siding.

Brian Morriso

230 An interior view of Orpington Depot, on 5th February 1984, once again showing EPB units. The two units in the distance are Class 415/1 sets Nos. 5032 and 5220, the latter having one nine-compartment trailer second car. No. 5322, in the foregroun (Class 415/2), is to a British Rail coach design, differing from those seen in *Plate 231* by, amongst other features, having flat nose ends and no electrical conduit on the roof.

Brian Morriso

31 On 5th February 1984, two Class 415/1 (4EPB) units, Nos. 5010 and 5177, stand in the 'down' sidings near the station. Differences again appear in the rain strip, which is located above the windows.

Brian Morrison

SEVENOAKS S.P.

232 The stabling point at Sevenoaks is situated south of the station near Sevenoaks Tunnel (1 mile 1,693 yards long). Again, EPB units are found alongside the wooden raised platforms at this location. On 5th February 1984, Nos. 5105 and 5016 could be found on the 'down' side of the main line, whilst in the distance, in the 'up' sidings, was No. 5202.

Brian Morrison

233 On 26th May 1963, Cl
33/2 'Slim Jims' Nos. D659
D6590 and D6592 sit outside t
old steam depot at Tonbridge. T
shed was situated south of the li
from Ashford to Redhill, and w
closed to steam around 196
although diesels used the buildi
after that date. The 4B headco
on No. D6590 indicates a worki
from Bricklayers Arms to Ore.

Peter Groo

234 The huge water-tower at Tonbridge Shed overlooks
Bulleid shunter No. 15225, on 9th March 1957. This locomotive was one of the last in the class to be withdrawn
from service, in November 1971, spending its final days
allocated to Selhurst Depot.

Frank Hornby

235 Tonbridge handles a large quantity of freight traffic,
including stone from the Foster Yeoman terminal. The
West Yard stables many locomotives, together with their
freight trains, and Class 73 electro-diesels and Class 33/2
'Slim Jims' make an interesting scene. On 3rd May 1978,
No. 73107 and four Class 33s await their next duty.

John Scrace

The Stabling Points

236 Between West Yard at Tonbridge and the main line to Redhill, diesel electric multiple units are stabled. A Class 203 (5L) unit, No. 1034, lies stabled in the sidings on 23rd June 1983. Of the original five, which excluded the buffet car included in the Class 202 (6L) units, only four 5L units now exist. *Colin J. Marsden*

237 A variety of units is stabled near Tonbridge Station and, on 5th February 1984, a Class 415/1 (4EPB) set, No. 5816, kept company with a Class 207 'East Sussex' diesel electric multiple unit, No. 1318, in the North Sidings, situated beside the Sevenoaks line.

Brian Morrison

238 Western Region-allocated diesel multiple units work into Tonbridge from Reading and Class 119 Gloucester RCW cross-country unit No. L581 is seen stabled in the station yard on 15th January 1984. On the side of the last two cars are the words 'Passenger Luggage Stowage Area' where conversion from guard's van space has taken place.

Rex Kennedy

TUNBRIDGE WELLS (West)

239 The fine 1866-built Tunbridge Wells (West) Station overlooks this major stabling point for diesel electric multiple units. On 15th January 1984 the yard was full with Class 205 (3H) 'Hampshire' sets and Class 207 (3D) 'East Sussex' sets, which is ironic, as Tunbridge Wells is in Kent. Those identifiable include Nos. 1107, 1315, 1110 and 1306. Diesel electric multiple units were first stabled at this location in 1962. The old steam shed, which officially closed to steam in 1963, can be seen beyond the ornate station buildings behind the platform.

Rex Kennedy

240 Looking away from the station at Tunbridge Wells (West), on 6th May 1980, we see Class 207 'East Sussex' unit No. 1308 near Grove Tunnel, where the line goes beneath the town and into Central Station. The Eridge line, on which Tunbridge Wells (West) Station is situated, has been threatened with closure for some time, and this would mean the closure of this fine station.

Brian Morrison

The Shed

241 Although Tunbridge Wells (West) Depot lost its allocation of steam locomotives in 1963, both steam and diesel traction were to be found there for some time afterwards. The building, as can be seen in *Plate 239*, still stands today and, on 11th June 1961, Class 33 No. D6522 was seen on shed amongst simmering steam locomotives which included a 4-4-0 Class D1, No. 31739 off Bricklayers Arms.

R. C. Riley

PADDOCK WOOD S.P.

242 Paddock Wood Station is the terminus of the line from Maidstone and, on 5th April 1979, Class 08 shunter No. 08811 was parked in the bay platform. At the time, the shunter was used for station pilot duties and, in the morning, at the Transfesa Terminal, situated at this location north of the line. It is seen attached to a Continental ferry van from this terminal.

Colin J. Marsden

MAIDSTONE (East) S.P.

243 The stabling point at Maidstone (East) Station is overlooked by the impressive court house and jail and, on 29th January 1984, a Class 414/3 (2HAP) unit, No. 6070, is seen at this location. This station is situated on the Swanley to Ashford line, and is one of three stations in the town.

Rex Kennedy

244 Class 73/1 No. 73101 *Brighton Evening Argus* is photographed whilst stabled at Faversham, on 6th June 1981. For the naming ceremony on 3rd December 1980, this locomotive carried the number 73100, indicating the newspaper's 100 years of circulation. It reverted to No. 73101 after the ceremony. In October 1981, No. 73101 met with an accident in Tonbridge Yard, causing considerable damage to the locomotive after running into a line of braked wagons. It was hauled to St. Leonards prior to extensive work being done at Eastleigh Works.

John Augustso.

245 This view of Faversham shows the complexity of track near the multiple unit stabling point where, generally, EPB units can be found. Class 415/1 (4EPB) set No. 5035 is pictured between the raised platforms, used for cleaning, and the modern signal box whilst another EPB unit is seen in the background. The lines from here to Dover, and to Ramsgate, first saw electrified services on 15th June 1959.

Colin J. Marsden

46 Electric multiple units are stabled at Margate near the station, and on 5th April 1984 two Class 414/3 (2HAP) units, Nos. 6172 and 6096, stand side by side and show that the headcode boxes differ in size, the smaller box indicating the later design. Beside the platform stands gangwayed throughout stock, a Class 411/5 unit, No. 1525 (formerly No. 7108).

Brian Morrison

47 On 15th April 1984, No. 1582, a Class 411/5 unit, stands in the platform at Margate Station. This platform has been set aside for upholstery and compartment repairs on electric multiple units. The present station at Margate dates from 1926 and replaced the original 1863 building.

Brian Morrison

48 This final view of the stabling point at Margate, shows a Class 423 (4VEP) unit, No. 7763, alongside 2HAP units, on 15th April 1984. The Ramsgate-based Class 423 units which, from time to time, are stabled at Margate, total approximately 27 sets, the majority of 4VEPs being allocated to Wimbledon, Brighton and Bournemouth.

Brian Morrison

249 A general view of a crowded Ramsgate Depot, pictured on Sunday, 27th February 1983. Refurbished Class 411/4 (4CEP) units are seen in abundance with Nos. 1525 and 1590 in the foreground, and another four on shed. Two more are stabled in the station siding and the monopoly is only broken by a solitary 2HAP unit and a Class 423 (4VEP) set.

Brian Morrison

250 On 27th February 1983, the station sidings at Ramsgate held two Class 423 (4VEP) units, Nos. 7894 and 7861, and a refurbished Class 411/4 (4CEP) unit, No. 1597. On refurbishment, all the 4CEP units received new numbers, No. 1597, prior to its conversion incorporating the inclusion of coaches from Class 410 (4BEP) units, being No. 7161.

Brian Morrison

252 Having arrived with stores o its weekly round, ex-2HAL unit now departmental set No. 022 stands on the depot reception road beside the brick and timber signal box which is situated near Ramsgate Station. No. 7177, since refurbishment to a Class 411/5 unit, now carries the number 1563, and i pictured standing in the station which handles approximately 200 trains each day from London.

Colin J. Marsden

251 The electric multiple unit depot at Ramsgate stands on the same site as the old steam depot, which closed in December 1960, a large depot abundant with an allocation of named steam locomotives of the 'Battle of Britain', 'West Country' and 'Schools' classes. Outside the now new steel structure, on 6th August 1979, stands Class 423 (4VEP) No. 7873 alongside a two car Class 414/3 (2HAP) unit, No. 6078, a class which is fast disappearing from the Southern Region scene. Sets of cleaning steps are also visible.

Colin J. Marsden

DOVER (Priory) S.P.

253 Dover (Priory) Station is situated on the line from Victoria, via Faversham, which is joined at Priory Station by the line from Ramsgate. It takes its name from the nearby St. Martin's Priory, and was opened in 1861. On 26th February 1984, a Class 419 motor luggage van, No. 68004, stands at this location beside the concrete walkway of the stabling point. All ten MLVs, Nos. 68001 to 68010, are based at Ramsgate, and they are regarded as light locomotives. They can change from live rail to battery power by the push of a button and, when on non-electrified lines, the collector shoes are pneumatically raised to avoid damage to them when returning to a live rail section.

Rex Kennedy

DOVER (Marine)

254 The four road depot at Dover (Marine), which is situated behind the wall of Western Docks Station, is pictured on 16th July 1978 and provides a selection of motive power. A Class 47 diesel, No. 47155, lies sandwiched between a Class 419 motor luggage van, No. 68001, and an un-refurbished 4CEP unit, No. 7205. Since refurbishment to a Class 411/5 unit, No. 7205 carries the number 1620. The entire fleet of MLVs work only on the South Eastern Division.

Stephen Charlson

DOVER (Western Docks) S.P.

255 A short distance away from Dover (Marine) is Dover Western Docks. Both diesel and electro-diesel locomotives can be found here, stabled in the yard, after having worked in with a variety of freight traffic. On 26th February 1984, a named Class 33 locomotive, No. 33052 *Ashford*, was accompanied by 'Slim Line' Class 33s Nos. 33206 and 33202.

Rex Kennedy

256 Standing beside a Continental Transfesa ferry van at Dover Western Docks, on 15th May 1982, is Class 73/1 electro-diesel No. 73112. It is noticeable that the ferry van has only a single air pipe. Trains from Western Docks Station pass the locomotives and rolling stock stabled at this location, whilst en route for Folkestone and Ashford, via Shakespeare and Abbotscliffe tunnels. The headcode '46' indicates a Victoria to Dover Marine, via Orpington, train.

John Augustson

257 A view looking down from the cliff top at the stabling point at Dover Western Docks. On 26th February 1984, a new-liveried Class 73, No. 73105, was seen stabled on a train beside dual-braked Class 09 shunter No. 09018, which was carrying out shunting operations at the time. The close proximity to the beach and sea are clearly visible, as are the roof details of the electro-diesel. This scene was photographed at the western end of the yard, near Shakespeare Tunnel.

Rex Kennedy

The Shed

258 Dover Shed (74C), which was situated at Western Docks, closed in 1961 after thirty three years of service. This view, taken in the shed yard on 24th September 1955, shows Class 08 shunter No. 13046 stabled with a steam locomotive. These 49 ton diesel-electric shunters were introduced in 1953 and were capable of a maximum speed of 20m.p.h. No. 13046 survived to become No. D3046, and can still be seen today as No. 08033 allocated to Sheffield (Tinsley).

Brian Morrison

SHEPHERDSWELL S.P.

259 Shepherdswell Station is situated at the north end of Lydden Tunnel, on the main Faversham to Dover line, and at the junction of the (freight only) East Kent Railway branch to Tilmanstone Quarry. Authority to use 350hp diesel shunters on this quarry branch, previously worked by ex-SR Class 01 0-6-0s, was given early in 1960 and, on 6th May 1960, Dover-allocated No. D3044 was given a trial over this line. On 18th August 1981, Class 09 shunter No. 09023 lay stabled at Shepherdswell Station, along with the brake van used on the branch. This particular brake van is air-piped with yellow panels on both sides and ends for identification purposes, and is marked 'Returned to Shepherds—Well'.
John Glover

FOLKESTONE S.P.

260 Three twelve car electric units, comprising a total of nine Class 411 (4CEP) units, are pictured on the stabling point at Folkestone, from above Martello Tunnel, on 26th February 1984. The units nearest the camera are Nos. 1503, 411508 and 411507. The stabling point is located beside the 'down' line to the east of Folkestone (East) Station, which can just be made out in the distance, further down the line. Full use will be made of these units on the following morning.
Andrew Kennedy

261 A ground level view of Folkestone stabling point, photographed on 26th February 1984, showing three Class 411 (4CEP) units, Nos. 411510, 1548 and 1599. The 4CEP units that were refurbished at Swindon Works from 1980 onwards, carry the 411 prefix to their numbers, as in No. 411510. Refurbishment provided new seating, tinted glass windows, lower ceilings and flourescent lighting.
Rex Kennedy

262 Ashford Shed closed to steam in 1963 but, prior to this, main line diesel locomotives were regularly to be found at this location. Amongst these were the Class 24s which were loaned from the London Midland Region in 1958, prior to the Kent Coast electrification. On 19th July 1959, No. D5017 is seen on shed in immaculate condition.

Peter Groom

263 On 20th May 1962, a Class 03 diesel-mechanical shunter, No. D2084, stands in the yard of the old steam depot at Ashford. Diesels were serviced at this depot until 1968, by which time part of the crumbling roof had been removed.

Peter Groom

267 Under the yard lights of Ashford Station stabling point, on 16th August 1979, stands Class 73/0 (JA) No. 73004, Class 33/2 'Slim Line' No. 33204 and Class 73/1 (JB) No. 73110. This front end view not only reveals the 'Slim Line's' narrow body but also shows the differing front end features of the electro-diesels. The Class 73/0 (JA) has an additional multiple control jumper beneath the driver's window

Colin J. Marsden

264 A Class 04 shunter, No. D2287, is seen at Ashford Shed on 4th September 1967. This locomotive only had one more month of working life before being withdrawn and scrapped by Pound Ltd. of Fratton. By the end of 1968, Ashford had lost its entire allocation of Class 04 shunters, except No. D2293 which lasted until being withdrawn in May 1971.

Peter Groom

265 One of the Bulleid shunters, No. 15228, rests in Ashford Shed Yard on 19th July 1959, and an old water column can be seen in the background. This shunter was built at Ashford and also spent its last days there. When entering service in 1951, No. 15228 was painted in the standard black livery and carried the lion on unicycle emblem, seen on the side.

Peter Groom

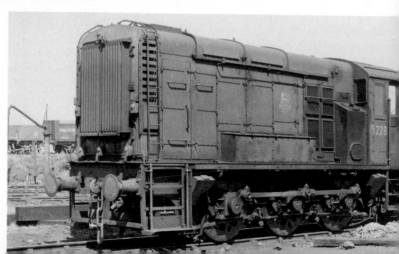

266 No. D6502, a Class 33 locomotive, pictured in the yard at Ashford on 25th March 1961, was the first locomotive in this class to be withdrawn. It was involved in a collision at Itchingfield Junction on 5th March 1964, which resulted in frame distortion, making the locomotive uneconomical to repair. It was eventually cut up at Eastleigh Works in July 1964.

Peter Groom

ASHFORD STATION S.P.

268 Class 71 straight electric No. E5011, showing its overhead pantograph system, lies stabled at Ashford Station stabling point on 5th September 1973. These locomotives spent their entire lives allocated to Ashford and were placed into store there in 1977 after almost twenty years of service, including heading the 'Night Ferry' and the prestigious 'Golden Arrow'.

Brian Morrison

ASHFORD (Chart Leacon)

269 Chart Leacon maintenance depot was built in 1961 on the 'up' side of the South Eastern Division's main line, about ¾ of a mile from the London side of Ashford Station. The depot, when built, was 496ft. long, 220ft. wide and 36ft. high. One of the 5 ton overhead travelling cranes is seen in this view, photographed on 5th September 1973, showing a Class 411 (4CEP) unit No. 7193 and a Class 423 (4VEP) unit No. 7723, both being serviced.

Brian Morrison

271 On 5th September 1973, work was being carried out at Chart Leacon Depot on Class 415 (4EPB) unit No. 5365, having been lifted from its bogies. A Class 205 'Hampshire' diesel electric unit, No. 1110, is also in for attention.

Brian Morrison

272 The running shed at Chart Leacon is pictured, on 5th September 1973, housing a Class 71 overhead electric locomotive, No. E5003. The running shed, also constructed in 1961, forms the fifth bay of the maintenance depot and on construction was 320ft. long and 69ft. 6in. wide. The inspection pits, on each of the four roads, were constructed to a length of 229ft. and all were provided with drainage, power points and bulkhead lighting.

Brian Morrison

273 This general view of the depot complex at Chart Leacon shows a variety of traction outside the buildings on 23rd July 1980. The Class 08 and 09 shunters are Nos. 08385, 08892, 08414 and 09013, and motor luggage van No. 68005 is seen in the background. A Class 423 (4VEP) unit stands on the near siding.

Barry Nicolle

270 Carrying the nameboard 'Waterloo' above the driver's side window, Class 430 (4REP) motor coach second car No. S62150, from set No. 3005, is lifted to have the front bogies removed at Chart Leacon Depot. Whilst a full mechanical overhaul takes place on the units, bogie frames are supersonically tested for internal flaws, and the wheels are turned on lathes. Brake block replacement is also necessary at regular intervals.

British Rail

274 St. Leonards provides two establishments; a British Rail running and maintenance depot for diesel electric multiple units, and also a CM&EE repair depot. Both these buildings can be seen in this view, photographed on 19th May 1982, and a Class 33 diesel lies stabled beside the CM&EE depot. Both depots are situated beside the main line from Hastings to Eastbourne, just west of Bopeep Tunnel and near the site of West Marina Station, which closed in 1967.

Rex Kennedy

275 On 8th January 1984, two Class 202 (6L) 'Hastings' diesel-electric units, Nos. 1017 and 1018, protrude into the afternoon sunshine from the maintenance depot at St. Leonards. The open front of this five road building, with its concrete walkways between the track, is clearly visible. All Class 201, 202, 203 and 207 diesel-electric units are allocated to St. Leonards, in addition to the majority of Class 205 sets, making its total allocation of this type of traction to well over 50 units.

Rex Kennedy

76 No. 1005, a Class 201 six car unit, stands over the inspection pits in the CM&EE repair depot at St. Leonards, on 8th January 1984. The first three Class 201 units were outshopped from Eastleigh Works by February 1957, and on one trial run, a speed of [7]5m.p.h. was attained up Micheldever Bank. Services using these 2,000 seated sets commenced on 17th June 1960, with twelve workings in each direction on weekdays, seventeen on Saturdays and eleven on Sundays, and with one rush hour service between Hastings and Cannon Street timed at 90 minutes.

Rex Kennedy

77 On 30th September 1979, No. 1206, the last Class 206 (3R) 'Tadpole' unit to be withdrawn, is pictured in the CM&EE repair depot at St. Leonards. By the end of the summer, in 1983, its power car, No. 60037, was in use as a spare vehicle in Class 201 'Hastings' sets and its trailer composite car, No. 60702, had been downgraded to a trailer second, and incorporated into Class 201 set, No. 1004. The Class 206 'Tadpole' units were formed in 1964 from ex-'Hastings' motor and trailer cars, and ex-electric multiple unit driving trailers, and were used on the Reading to Redhill line.

Colin J. Marsden

278 Class 33/0 locomotive No. 33005 stands outside the CM&EE repair depot at St. Leonards on 29th August 1982. The new modern depot, built to house and maintain the new diesel electric multiple units, was opened early in 1957, to coincide with the first deliveries. In 1963, all the 'Slim Line' Class 33/2 locomotives were allocated to this depot, but by 1958, all had been moved to Hither Green.

Andrew French

The Old Steam Shed

279 Although the old steam depot at St. Leonards officially closed in June 1958, diesel locomotives were stabled inside the depot into the early 1960s. This depot was situated on the other side of the line to the present depot complex and was directly opposite West Marina Station. A solitary Class 33 diesel is seen inside the old steam depot.

W. T. Stubbs Collection

HASTINGS S.P.

280 Diesel electric multiple uni of St. Leonards Depot are stable in a siding beside the line, betwee Hastings Station and Ore. As ca be seen in this view, the main li at this point is double track, b beyond Mount Pleasant Tunne seen in the distance, it is sing track as far as Appledore. On 8t January 1984, Class 202 'Hastin six car unit, No. 1013, is picture at this location.

Andrew Kennea

STREATHAM HILL S.P.

281 The stabling point at Streatham Hill lies to the south of the line from Clapham Junction to Beckenham Junction, and east of Streatham Hill Station. Four sidings, with raised concrete walkways for cleaning, make up this location and, on 5th March 1981, Class 421/2 (4CIG) units, Nos. 7397 and 7399, together with Class 421/1 (4CIG) unit No. 7335, and Class 415/1 (4EPB) unit No. 5006, virtually fill the area.

Colin J. Marsden

BECKENHAM JUNCTION S.P.

282 On 18th April 1984, a Class 415/1 (4EPB) unit, No. 5014, stands in the Central Division's stabling point at Beckenham Junction Station. The platform at which it stands, is no longer used for passengers, and this stabling point is now only used on Sundays.

Brian Morrison

NORWOOD JUNCTION

◀

284 Norwood Junction had its fair share of proto type diesels and, on 18th May 1957, No. 11001, the Bulleid-designed, Ashford-built, 0-6-0 diesel shunter stood at the old steam depot. When introduced in 1950, this locomotive was designed not only as a yard and hump shunter, but also for inter-yard trips. Its 12ft. 6in. wheelbase was designed to negotiate 4 chain curves, and its 600 gallon fuel tanks are located at the front of the locomotive. Although 4ft longer than the standard Class 08 shunter of today, No. 11001 was only a shade heavier, at 49 tons 9 cwt.

John Faulkner

285 Another early diesel locomotive which was allocated to Norwood Junction in the days of steam was No. 10800, pictured outside the depot on 18th April 1953. This locomotive carried out its first official demonstration on 14th November 1950, from Euston to Watford, and it was originally designed for cross-country and branch line work. By 1952, No. 10800 was working a Brighton Section duty from Norwood Junction, involving a daily round trip of 302¼ miles (322 miles on Wednesdays and Saturdays). It was later used on pick-up goods trains.

Jim Aston ▶

283 The old steam depot at Norwood Junction was situated to the north of Norwood Junction Station, about a mile from the present day washing plant and stabling point, and near Bromley Junction. The depot closed is 1964 and was demolished in 1966. On 11th August 1963, the selection of shunters and Class 33 diesels seem to outnumber the steam locomotives. As can be seen in this view, this location, even in its latter days, was still an impressive sight.

John Scrace

286 Southern No. 3 was one of the three shunters built by the Southern Railway in 1937, and it eventually became No. 15203 after 1948. It is seen at Norwood Junction on 3rd June 1939, in pre-nationalisation days. No. 3 was, in fact, the very first diesel locomotive to work at Hither Green Depot where it was used for trials, with Norwood Junction receiving an SR Class Z 0-8-0T, No. 951, whilst it was on loan from them.

Norman Preedy Collection

287 The same diesel shunter as that shown in *Plate 286*, with its revised number. Photographed at Norwood Junction on 21st July 1963, it shows the other side of the locomotive, and carries the ladder at the front end. No. 15203 spent its final days allocated to Selhurst, was withdrawn in December 1964, and was broken up by Hayes at Bridgend.

Peter Groom

288 Three Ashford-built shunters of the 1949—1952 period stand beside the old steam depot at Norwood Junction. No. 15211 leads the trio and was the first to come from the works early in 1949. Their 4ft. 6in. driving wheels and 17½ : 1 gear ratio permitted speeds up to 27m.p.h., unlike those previously-built shunters of the LMR and WR which had only been capable of 20m.p.h. They were also fitted with an automatic cut-out to guard against exceeding the new speed limit.

Lens of Sutton

289 By standing on the road bridge at Tennison Road, SE 25, one can look north, to view Norwood Junction Station and the present day stabling point, and south to see Selhurst Depot. This view of Norwood Junction, photographed on 5th March 1982, shows (on the right) Class 73/0 electro-diesel No. 73005, and Class 33 No. 33062 arriving from the main line, whilst on the left are two Class 33s, Nos. 33044 and 33063, and a Class 73, No. 73142 *Broadlands*, stabled in the sidings.

Colin J. Marsden

The Stabling Poin

290 The washing machine at No wood Junction is officially called th Selhurst washer and, on 6th Apr 1978, a Class 205 (3H) diesel electr multiple unit, No. 1114, passe through for its regular 'wash and brus up'. These units are not allocated t Selhurst Depot, but receive mainten ance there when required.

Colin J. Marsde

291 With Selhurst Depot in the distance, three 0-6-0 diesel shunters stand by, whilst Class 09 No. 09009 works the yard at Norwood Junction on 6th April 1978. This is the view that one sees from the other side of Tennison Road bridge, and shows where the Norwood Junction section ends and the Selhurst Section commences. An abundance of units can be seen, from Selhurst Depot, on the right, through to the yards in the centre background.

Brian Morrison

292 Showing the standard Selhurst shed code (SU) on its cabside, and the distinctive gap which once appeared between the second and third digits of the locomotive's number, Class 09 shunter No. 09015 awaits attention in Selhurst Depot on 17th September 1980.

Graham Scott-Lowe

293 Unusually carrying the shed code SHST above the front steps, Class 08 shunter No. 08158 is pictured over the inspection pit, inside Selhurst Depot on 26th January 1975. This code was not usually found on the Selhurst shunters and the locomotive is now withdrawn.

Norman Preedy

294 At Selhurst Depot, the motor open brake second car from 4SUB unit No. 4125 undergoes conversion to de-icing unit No. 009. Extensive work is being carried out and the new slimmer end windows have already been fitted. Together with other modifications, the conversion also entails the sealing up of all but two doors in the former seating bays of the coach and also the driver's doors, access to the cab then being via the adjoining brake van.

Colin J. Marsden

295 On 21st September 1980, one of the first Class 415/1 (4EPB) units to be refurbished, stands inside Selhurst Depot. No. 5143, in its refurbished state, only carried this number for about three months prior to being reclassified 415/4 and being renumbered 5403. Before refurbishment, 4EPB units generally only carried the number once at each end, over the headcode box *(see Plate 230)*. Alongside stands Gloucester RCW Class 119 diesel multiple unit No. L588, a unit used on the Reading to Tonbridge line, strangely carrying the destination 'Hereford' on the blind.

John Glover

296 General overhaul on Waterloo and City stock is now carried out at Selhurst but, at one time, this took place at Eastleigh. At an 'open day' at Selhurst on 17th September 1980, Waterloo and City Class 487 power car No. S59 is seen, minus bogies, in the workshops awaiting repair. There are maintenance facilities at Selhurst for locomotives, diesel units and electric units, and no repair is beyond their scope. A new maintenance depot at Selhurst, for electric multiple units, is to be built on the site of the disused stabling sidings near Norwood Fork Junction. This will replace the existing depot at Selhurst which dates from 1926, and it is anticipated that the new depot will be operative by 1986.

Graham Scott-Lowe

297 Standing on the scrap line at Selhurst, in September 1979, is Class 405 (4SUB) unit No. 4753, and an ex-2HAL set converted to form the Selhurst de-icing unit, No. 018. The de-icing units formed from 2HAL sets, are being replaced by ex-4SUBs to form a new fleet of departmental stock.

Colin J. Marsden

298 The 'open day' at Selhurst on 17th September 1980, provided an interesting display of visiting motive power, which had been specially brought in for the occasion. Alongside the depot are Class 50 No. 50023 *Howe,* Class 47 No. 47581 *Great Eastern,* Class 31 No. 31112 and Class 33/0 No. 33056 *The Burma Star,* and all helped to make the day a success.

Graham Scott-Lowe

ADDISCOMBE S.P.

299 Addiscombe Station is at the end of the branch line from Elmers End, which leaves the main line at Woodside Junctio
There is just one double-sided platform at Addiscombe and in this view, photographed on 6th April 1978, a Class 415/1 (4EP
unit, No. 5187, is stabled at the platform on the left, whilst other stock is being cleaned in preparation for its next duty.

Brian Morriso

300 On 9th February 1984, a Class 416/1 (2EPB) unit lay stabled in the sidings at Epsom, which are situated at the junctio
of the lines from Wimbledon and Sutton. No. 5677, seen here, is one of a batch of units built in 1958 to replace ageing uni
on the Waterloo, Windsor and Weybridge lines. Epsom Station, seen in the background, is scheduled for redevelopment, whic
will provide new booking hall facilities and many other improvements.

John Glov

EPSOM S.P.

301 Three EPB units stand at Tattenham Corner Station on 28th March 1980. Class 415/1 (4EPB) No. 5002 and Class 416/1 (2EPB) No. 5652 are stabled, whilst between them, Class 416/1 (2EPB) No. 5666 prepares to leave with the 16.03 train to London Bridge. In January 1963, due to severe winter conditions, electric services on this branch had to be replaced by steam-hauled trains. The most interesting working to Tattenham Corner every year is the locomotive-hauled 'Royal Train', on Derby Day.

Brian Morrison

COULSDEN (North) S.P.

302 Class 405 (4SUB) unit No. 4732 stands beside one of the raised concrete walkways at Coulsden (North) stabling point on 6th July 1979. No. 4732 had the distinction of being painted in the Southern green livery *(see Plate 95)*. Coulsden (North) Station, which only provided a peak hour service, closed in October 1983 resulting in the operating of a new suburban service to Smitham, nearby, on the Tattenham Corner branch. The stabling point, therefore, is no longer required.

Colin J. Marsden

303 A scene from the past. Five electric units of types 4SUB and 2SAP, all now condemned, stand on a stabling siding which has now been lifted, at Coulsden (North) on 6th July 1979. The Class 405 (4SUB) units are Nos. 4277, 4742, 4719 and 4750, and the Class 418 (2SAP) unit is No. 5625.

Colin J. Marsden

Pre-Nationalisatio

304 This view of Coulsden (Nor stabling point, as it was when pho graphed on 28th May 1927, altho in Southern Railway days, was worthy of inclusion in this volu It shows LB&SCR overhead stock the motor van (generally known as milk van) is the third vehicle in train. The Coulsden (North)/Sut extensions were worked by 21 mo vans, 60 driving trailers and 20 trail These trains normally operated in car sets but, at times, two sets wor in multiple.

H. C. Casser

305 The milk van seen in the train in *Plate 304* is featured in this view, in close up. These unusually-designed vehicles were virtually electric locomotives and there were driving cabs at each end with the guard's van in between. After the Southern Railway opted to abandon the overhead pick-up system for third rail, in the late 1920s, the milk vans were converted at Eastleigh into goods brakes.

H. C. Casserley

06 Caterham Station, as viewed from the multi-storey car-park, on 26th January 1984. The station is being renovated and only the nearside platform is used by service trains. Stabled beyond are Class 415/4 (4EPB) units Nos. 5421 and 5425.

Brian Morrison

OXTED S.P.

07 A Class 205 'Hampshire' diesel electric multiple unit, No. 1106, is seen stabled in the siding at Oxted on 25th April 1978. It bears the four letter code (SLEO) for St. Leonards at the brake van end. Diesel electric units in the form of Class 207 (3D) 'East Sussex' sets were first tried out from St. Leonards Depot to Oxted in April 1962, but as production of the units was behind schedule, owing to a large staff exodus from Eastleigh Carriage Works after the official announcement of plans to close it, these units did not enter service on the line until after the commencement of the summer 1962 timetable.

Graham Wise

308 A bird's-eye view of the depot area Redhill, photographed on 29th March 197 Both unit stock and locomotives can be see This is the site of the old steam shed whi closed to steam in 1965, but retained i buildings for another four years. The uni stand roughly in the area of the old she building, and the turntable was in the vici ity of the Class 33 locomotive seen in th foreground. The station is in the distanc and the line on the right goes to Tonbridge.

John Scra

310 Beside Redhill's old steam depot, on September 1968, stands Class 09 shunter No. D It is photographed prior to being fitted wit brakes.

Robert Pri

309 Electric and diesel traction lie stabled at Redhill on 15th April 1982. Class 33/0 No. 33045 slightly obscures the view of Class 73/1 No. 73142 *Broadlands*.

John Scrace

311 The Selhurst-allocated shunter which operates at Redhill is to be found adjacent to the station when off duty and, on 29th Ja 1984, Class 09 No. 09003, in ex-works condition, was to be fou this location.

Rex Ker

12 Dorking Station lies on the Leatherhead to Horsham line, just north of the point where the Guildford to Redhill line crosses from east to west. The large stabling point for electric units is beside the station to the west of the line and, on 29th January 1984, it was home for Class 455 units. The first of these units entered service in March 1983, on the South Western Division, chiefly to replace the ageing 4SUB units, and to enable the three year old Class 508 sets to be transferred to Merseyside.

Rex Kennedy

13 On 29th January 1984, the monopoly of Class 455 units was broken by a solitary Class 415/6 refurbished 4EPB set, No. 5326, now carrying the number twice at each end. It was seen beside the raised concrete ramp of the stabling point.

Rex Kennedy

314 Prior to the introduction of the Class 455 units on the Dorking services, this location played host to Class 405 (4SUB) units. On 15th September 1979, the stabling point was almost full, and those standing off duty included Nos. 4631, 4626 and 4633.

Colin J. Marsden

316 Although the main attraction for the railway enthusiast, since May 1984, has been the new 'Gatwick Express' trains, at Gatwick, both electric and diesel units are still to be found stabled at this location. On 28th May 1984, a Class 119 Gloucester RCW set, No. L594, with car No. W51104 leading, stands beside Class 423 (4VEP) units Nos. 7812 and 7790. The diesel unit has probably worked in from Redhill, and the main Brighton line passes the stabling point.

Brian Morrison

THREE BRIDGES

317 On 3rd June 1960, electric locomotive No. 20001 is seen at Three Bridges. It was first numbered CC1 and left Ashford Works in 1941, two years before a second similar locomotive, No. CC2. It was originally designed for freight work but, by May 1968, had graduated to working the 'Royal Train' on Derby Day, from Victoria to Tattenham Corner.

Terry Gough

318 Standing at the buffers on a siding at Three Bridges Depot, on 22nd April 1963, is Class 71 straight electric locomotive No. E5013. This locomotive was not one of the ten which were converted to Class 74 electro-diesels.

Peter Groom

➤

315 Class 405 (4SUB) unit No. 4638 shivers in the snow of December 1978 at Dorking stabling point. It carries the headcode '17', indicating a Waterloo service.

John Vaughan

319 This view of the old steam shed at Three Bridges, shows Class 33 diesels intermingled with steam traction. The building dates from 1909 and was of brick, with a 'northlight' pattern roof, and had a water-tower nearby. In 1963 Three Bridges received its first allocation of Class 33 diesels, and in 1964 the depot closed to steam.

W. T. Stubbs Collection

320 On 28th September 1968, Class 73/1 electro-diesel No. E6047 stands at Three Bridges stabling point, near the derelict buildings. On 1st November 1982, David Kirby, the General Manager of the Southern Region, unveiled a plaque at Three Bridges to commemorate 50 years of operation of Britain's pioneer main line electric power supply control room, which opened there in July 1932.

Robert Pritchard

321 The Southern Region's experimental push-pull set, No. 601, is pictured at Three Bridges Depot. The set, classified 6TC, is made up of ex-6PUL trailer coaches and ex-4COR motor coaches. After push-pull trials, it entered service in 1966, with specially-converted Class 33 locomotive No. D6580, on the Oxted line. It was later transferred to the Clapham Junction to Kensington Olympia service and, after a collision, was withdrawn.

Duncan Simmonds

322 One of the unit stabling points at Horsham is situated beside the station. On 15th January 1984, EPB units filled this location, and in the foreground is a Class 415/1 (4EPB) unit, No. 5113. This stabling point was once filled with 4SUB units, and on 11th July 1983, the last scheduled South Western Division 4SUB working left Horsham at 06.56 for Waterloo.

Rex Kennedy

323 North of Horsham Station, beside the Crawley line, is another stabling point and, on 15th January 1984, this unique 4TEP unit, No. 2701, was seen at this location. This set is a refurbished Class 411 (4CEP) unit which, in place of its trailer open second car, incorporates a Class 410 (4BEP) buffet car. Alongside stood a Class 423 (4VEP) unit, No. 7878.

Rex Kennedy

324 An unusual visitor to the Crawley line stabling point at Horsham, on 19th February 1983, was Class 47 No. 47547, which stood at the head of its air-conditioned stock, before forming a diverted 09.36 Horsham to Manchester (Piccadilly) train. This, in fact, is normally the Brighton to Manchester train.

John Vaughan

325 Electric locomotive No. 20003 had more box-like look about it than Nos. 2000 and 20002. The pantograph on the roof wa used where overhead electric current was avai able, and in goods yards where third rail electr fication was dangerous to railway staff. Nc 20003 is seen at Horsham on 14th April 1963.

John Scrad

326 A Class 09 shunter, No. 09026 (formerly No. 4114) is seen stabled in Haywards Heath Station yard on 23rd May 1976. Although this location is near Brighton, this was a Selhurst-based shunter which, later in the year, was transferred to Bournemouth.

Norman Preedy

UCKFIELD S.P.

327 Uckfield stabling point, on 8th October 1983, and Class 33 No. 33048 stands berthed with the stock of a London Bridge to Eridge 'Chartex' train beside a Class 205 'Hampshire' unit, No. 1110. The unit is about to leave for London. Uckfield is now a terminus for trains from London Bridge, but was once an intermediate station on the Tunbridge Wells to Brighton line.

John Vaughan

28 This fine view of the stabling point at Bognor, photographed on 21st January 1984, shows its situation beside the terminus station. Standing off duty is a Class 420 (4BIG) unit, and on the right is a Class 421 (4CIG) unit, No. 7388. Another 4CIG unit, No. 7368, has 'the road' and forms a Bognor to Victoria train.

John Vaughan

29 Barnham lies at the junction where the Bognor branch leaves the main Portsmouth to Brighton line. On 23rd January 1982, two units were stabled for the weekend, Class 421/2 (4CIG) No. 7399, and Class 416/2 (2EPB) No. 5783 (ex-Tyneside stock). Passing, on service, is Class 420 (4BIG) unit No. 7051 forming a Victoria to Bognor train.

Brian Morrison

BARNHAM S.P.

LITTLEHAMPTON

330 On 4th December 1983, a Class 421/1 (4CIG) unit, No. 7304, occupied the corrugated shed building at Littlehampton. Electrified services to Littlehampton commenced on 3rd July 1938, on the same date as those from Barnham to Bognor. The depot is situated beside the 'up' line, about one mile from Littlehampton Station.

Rex Kennedy

331 Between the depot building and the station, at Littlehampton, a stabling point for units is situated beneath the gasometer and beside the 'down' line. On 4th December 1983, Class 413/3 (4CAP) unit No. 3301, stands off duty at this location. This unit was converted from Class 414 (2HAP) units, Nos. 6055 and 6057. The Class 414 (2HAP) units which were not so converted, were all withdrawn due to the 'asbestos' regulations *(see Plate 191)*.

Rex Kennedy

WEST WORTHING

332 There are three stations at Worthing but the electric unit depot is situated adjacent to West Worthing Station. The three roads each house a twelve car commuter set, and all leave the depot for London in the early morning and return in the early evening. Standing between the semaphore signals and the 1938-built shed building, early in 1984, are three Class 421 (4CIG) formations.

John Vaughan

333 This view of West Worthing Depot shows the interior with just one twelve car set, headed by Class 421 (4CIG) unit No. 7381, taking up residence on the inner road, on 4th December 1983. All units using this depot are allocated to Brighton.

Rex Kennedy

334 This 1969 view of West Worthing Depot shows a 4VEP unit, No. 7710, in an unusual livery of blue with a small yellow warning panel, leading a morning twelve car Littlehampton to London Bridge train. On shed, is a 4COR unit and a 4CIG set, and beside it, a green 2BIL unit makes up the trio. The variety of multiple unit classes has now sadly disappeared from this location.

John Vaughan

335 On a cold winter's day in 1965, a very clean green-liveried Class 33, No. D6572, trundles into the old Brighton steam shed. Note the lion and wheel BR emblem and the oil lamp on the leading lamp bracket. The locomotive is seen passing the water softening plant, situated beside the water-tower which has a clock on the wall. The buildings in the background comprise the carriage cleaning shed. Brighton Shed became 'all diesel' from 6th January 1964, although steam locomotives were still serviced there until the withdrawal of the steam-hauled Horsham to Brighton service.

John Vaughan

336 Early in 1953, the LMS prototype Co-Co diesel No 10001 reached the Southern Region, initially to work Waterloo to Exeter services and the Bournemouth line. The LMS was the first to produce a main line diesel, although the idea first came to the Southern. Whilst on the Southern Region, No. 10001 was overhauled at Brighton, and it is pictured on shed, at this location, on 2nd October 1954. No. 10001, together with Nos. 10000 and 10201 to 10203 was transferred back to the London Midland Region early in 1955.

Brian Morrison

Shunters at Brighton

337 No. D2082, a Class 03 shunter, pictured at Brighton Shed, on 9th April 1960 was, at that time, the only one of its class allocated to Brighton and, in fact, only three other members of the class, around this period, were allocated to the Southern Region; Nos. D2083 (73C), D2084 (73F) and D2085 (71A).

Peter Groom

338 One of the differences between the two Gardner-engined 204hp 0-6-0 diesel shunters, the Class 03 and the Class 04, was the wheel diameter. The smaller-wheeled Class 04 had 3ft. 3in. wheels, whereas the 03s were fitted with those of 3ft. 7½in. diameter. On 9th April 1960, when this view was photographed, Brighton had an allocation of three Class 04 shunters, and No. D2281 is pictured on shed.

Peter Groom

339 The interior of Brighton (Lovers' Walk) electric multiple unit maintenance depot has, on occasions, been used for the stabling of locomotives. Two locally-allocated Class 03 shunters, Nos. D2003 and D2030, are seen on 28th September 1968, standing over the inspection pit, and a glimpse of electric locomotive No. 20002, the second locomotive of this type, which left Ashford Works in 1943 as No. CC2, can be seen behind them.

Robert Pritchard

340 The brick-built facade of roads 6 to 12 of Brighton (Lovers' Walk) Depot is clearly seen in this view of 4th December 1983, showing No. 7366, a Class 421/2 (4CIG) unit, protruding from the entrance to road No. 9. On 16th July 1983, two of these 4CIG units, Nos. 7363 and 7364 joined forces to make an attempt at a record breaking run from London Bridge to Brighton, to commemorate 50 years of electrification on the Brighton line. The run was completed in a record time of 41 minutes 38 seconds, beating the previous record by 7 minutes and 3 seconds.

Rex Kennedy

341 On 4th December 1983, Class 423 (4VEP) unit No. 7801 stands at temporary blocks in Brighton's maintenance depot. It is photographed in that part of the building which houses roads 1 to 5, and a greater degree of natural light shines through its roof, unlike that of roads 6 to 12.

Rex Kennedy

344 For many years, locomotives have been stabled under the shelter of Brighton Station, between platforms 2 and 3, especially at weekends. During 1969, two of the Bulleid-designed Ashford-built Co-Co electric locomotives, Nos. 20001 and 20003, were seen at this location. No. 20003, built in 1948, was more powerful than No. 20001 which was outshopped from Ashford as No. CC1 in 1941, and No. 20003 was also heavier by 5 tons. Soon after this picture was taken, these locomotives were withdrawn, because as they were non-standard, this resulted in long delays in obtaining spares, and they required special attention when being serviced.►

John Vaughan

343 At the end of Brighton Station, a line is used at times for the stabling of units and, on 4th December 1983, Class 413/2 (4CAP) set No. 3212 is pictured here. Partially due to the variable location of van space on certain 'Coastway' services, it was suggested that Brighton-based Class 414 (2HAP) units be permanently coupled, formed into 4CAP units, and renumbered accordingly. No. 3212, seen here, is formed of ex-2HAP units Nos. 6014 and 6041.

Rex Kennedy

342 The metal-faced frontage of the depot at Lovers' Walk, Brighton, which houses roads 1 to 5, is clearly visible in this view, taken on 4th December 1983, showing Class 423 (4VEP) No. 7807 at the entrance. The contrast between this part of the shed and that of roads 6 to 12 beside it is clearly visible.

Rex Kennedy

345 On 4th December 1983, a Class 33 locomotive stands in the yard outside Lovers' Walk Depot at Brighton. This yard lies just beyond the end of the station platforms, and is the regular stabling point for the main line diesels and electro-diesels which have worked into Brighton on passenger and freight services. The headcode '35' indicates a semi-fast London Bridge to Brighton, via Redhill, train.

Rex Kennedy

346 The maximum speed of the Class 73/1 (JB) electro-diesels is 90m.p.h. as against the 80m.p.h. of the Class 73/0 (JA) version. Two Class 73/1 (JB) electro-diesels, Nos. 73112 and 73106, lie stabled adjacent to Brighton Station together with a Class 33 on 4th December 1983. The station buildings, seen in the background, were originally designed by David Moccatta, but changes, including the erection of the arched roof, occurred in 1882/3. The station opened in May 1840 for trains to Shoreham and in September 1841 for LB&SCR services to London.

Rex Kennedy

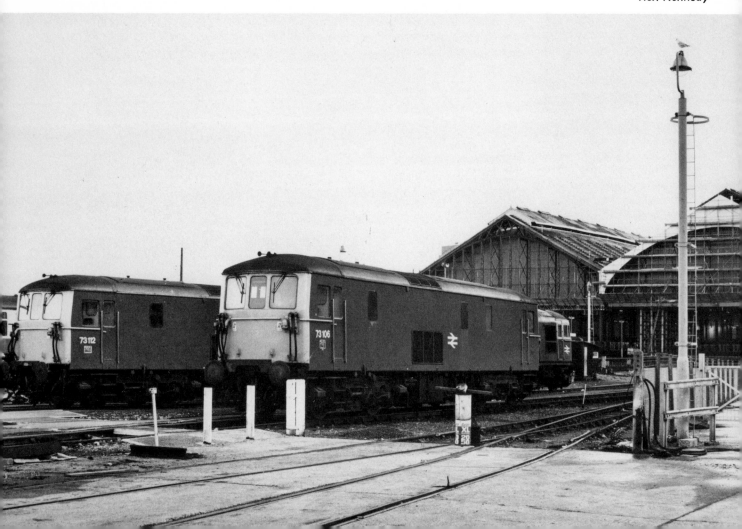

SEAFORD S.P.

347 Seaford lies at the end of the line from Lewes which, from Newhaven, is single line only. The station opened on 1st June 1864, and on 23rd January 1982, a Class 423 (4VEP) unit, No. 7731, is seen stabled at this location. Occasionally, Class 413/2 (4CAP) units are also stabled here.

Brian Morrison

348 In 1965, Newhaven was transformed into Britain's most modern car ferry terminal, and the terminal area is shown in this view. Lying stabled at Newhaven Marine Station, on 8th January 1984, with a large ship visible alongside, is a Class 421/2 (4CIG) set, No. 7431, coupled with a similar unit. The sea crossing from here to Dieppe is longer than that from Dover to Calais, but Dieppe is nearer to Paris and the French coastal resorts.

Rex Kennedy

NEWHAVEN S.P.

349 A Selhurst-allocated shunter could, until recent years, be found stabled at weekends near the Newhaven to Seaford road bridge, which is adjacent to Newhaven Town Station. On 16th December 1979, a Class 09, No. 09012, taking a rest from working the yard, is seen at this location.

Dawlish Warren Railway Museum

350 At Eastbourne Station, multiple unit stabling points are at both the centre of the station complex, near the platforms, and also beside the 'up' line. On 8th January 1984, Class 421 (4CIG) units are seen stabled here. Electrification reached Eastbourne in 1935 and just north of the station, at Willingdon Junction, lines from Lewes and Hastings converge prior to the run into Eastbourne.

Rex Kennedy

351 On 27th July 1982, Class 421/2 (4CIG) unit No. 7368 moves off Ore Depot to form the 18.22 Ore to Victoria train. The depot is situated behind the 'up' platform at Ore and the wooden ticket office and waiting-room are seen on the left of the picture. This four road shed offers servicing facilities for Central Division electric unit stock and the station, situated in the South Eastern Division, receives services from Victoria, Brighton and Ashford.

Brian Morrison

ORE

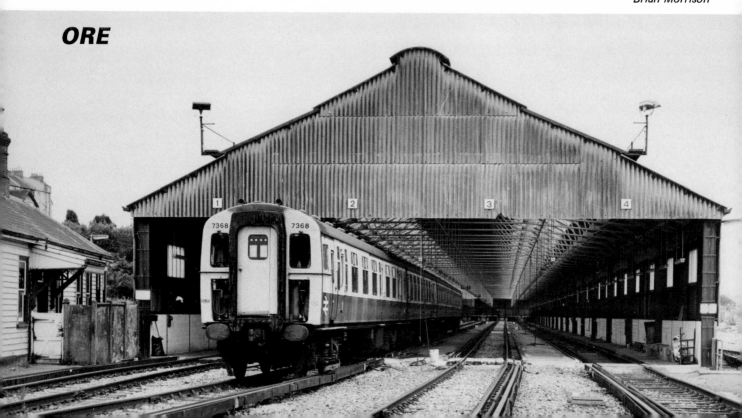